TAROT AND THE

OF THE HERO

TAROT

and the

JOURNEY

of the

HERO

HAJO BANZHAF

SAMUEL WEISER, INC.
York Beach, Maine

First published in 2000 by
SAMUEL WEISER, INC.
Box 612
York Beach, Maine 03910-0612

Library of Congress Cataloging-in-Publication Data

Banzhaf, Hajo.
   [Tarot und die Reise des Helden. English]
   Tarot and the journey of the hero / Hajo Banzhaf.
      p. cm.
   Includes bibliographical references and index.
   ISBN 0-57863-117-3 (alk. paper)
   1. Tarot. 2. Heroes—Miscellanea. I. Title.
   BF1879.T2B36513 2000
   133.3'2424—dc21   99-059294
                                     CIP

Translated by Christine M. Grimm
Cover and text design by Kathryn Sky-Peck
Typeset in 12 point Adobe Garamond

PRINTED IN CHINA BY TOPPAN PRINTING CO., LTD.

06 05 04 03 02 01 00
7   6   5   4   3   2   1

Contents

List of Illustrations

Acknowledgments

I THANK SALLIE NICHOLS, AN AMERICAN JUNGIAN depth psychologist, for her inspiration. Her profound book, *Jung and Tarot* (published by Samuel Weiser in 1980), drew my attention to the mythological background of the tarot cards many years ago. Through her, it became clear to me that the journey of the hero assumes a vivid form in the tarot. I am very thankful to her for this. Since then, the path her book opened up for me has not let go of me. Recognizing the archetypal symbols in the 22 cards of the major arcana on the path of a human being's life—and understanding these with increasing depth—has been among the most enriching experiences of my life.

Just as much I want to thank Helmut Remmler, founder and head of the C. G. Jung Institute in Munich, who guided me for many years and helped me understand the meaning of so many symbols as finger-boards on my path and in the everyday life. He would have written the preface to this book, but he died too early.

I also want to thank Stuart Kaplan of U.S. Games Systems, Inc., for allowing me to reproduce cards from the Universal-Waite Tarot deck and the Tarot of Marseilles in this book. He has been very helpful to me over the years—and to anyone looking into the imagery of the tarot cards.

And last but not least, I thank that mysterious lady dressed in black who gave me an appointment at the midnight hour more than 20 years ago when I saw the tarot cards for the first time in my life. She was a Polish Jew and stayed in Munich not for long. I do not know her name nor where she is now. Looking back from now, our meeting turned out to be a crossroad that has changed my life completely.

WHAT IS
TAROT?

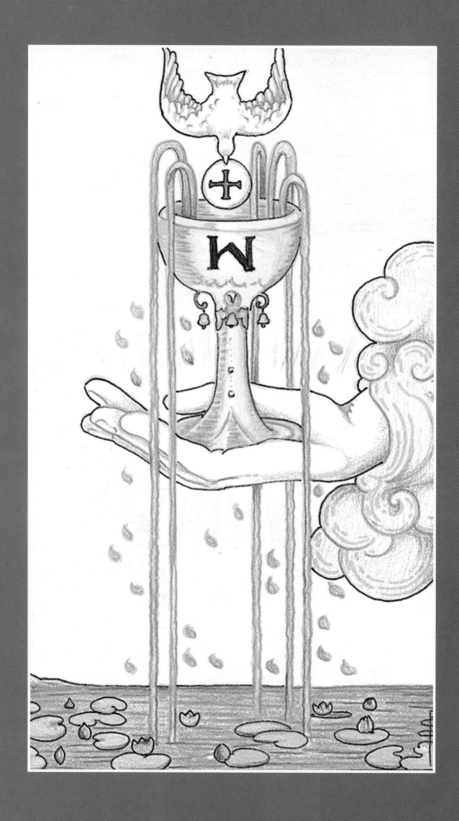

T he tarot is an oracle that has been used since the 16th century. It consists of a pack of 78 cards that are divided into two main groups: one group of 22 cards, the major arcana,[1] and the 56 cards of the minor arcana. While the major arcana is composed of 22 individual motifs in which there are no repetitions, and which form a clear sequence on the basis of their numbering, those of the minor arcana—the precursors of our modern playing cards—are divided into four suits: Wands, Swords, Cups, and Pentacles, from which Clubs, Spades, Hearts, and Diamonds later developed. Each series begins—as in the playing cards—with an Ace and then continues with 2, 3, up to the 10 as the highest card. In addition, there are the respective court cards: King, Queen, Knight, and Page. This means that there is one card more than is customary for modern playing cards.

Origin, Structure, and Symbolism of the Cards

Whether these two groups originally belonged together, or have only found each other over the course of time, is just as uncertain as the origin of the cards. Evidence has been found supporting the assumption that the cards of the minor arcana came to Europe from the Islamic world during the 14th century. But what was seen on these cards and what people did with them—whether they had an oracular value, or were purely playing cards, is not known. We know even less about the origin of the major arcana cards, which are much more significant to people familiar with the tarot. They appeared around the year 1600, and the assumptions about their origin differ greatly, like quite a few other things about the tarot. Some people conclude that the cards were initially created around 1600 because they first appeared around 1600; another group assumes that with the major arcana they are holding no less than the Book of Wisdom of the ancient Egyptian priest caste in their hands, which reached Europe in a mysterious way from ancient Egypt.

Among the many imaginative stories centered on the tarot cards is the speculation that they came to Palestine with the exodus of the people of Israel through Moses, for Moses was initiated into the Egyptian

---

[1] Latin *arkanum*—"secret," *arkana*—"secrets."

mysteries as a High Priest. Once the cards arrived in Palestine, they became connected with the Cabala, the secret Jewish teaching that recognizes a deep symbolic value in the 22 letters of the Hebraic alphabet, among other things. The numerological correspondences of the 22 letters of this alphabet with the 22 cards of the major arcana is among the weightiest evidence for this presumption about their origin. However, in this context one should know that many other things composed of 22 components have already been related to the tarot, such as the Gospel of St. John,[2] which includes 22 chapters. In this process, the pure wish often appears to have been the father of perception. The frequently complicated mental acrobatics required to substantiate the correlations claimed are then interpreted as evidence that this is a true secret doctrine.

Cynthia Giles comments on these efforts in her insightful tarot book:

> Among the authors who lay claim special knowledge, each is careful to distinguish himself from those "others," whose lay false claim to the truth, or who know only a portion of the *real* truth. The secret nature of their claimed knowledge . . . has automatically exempted them from the necessity of proving or supporting their stories. So, in the final analysis, there is not one whit of reason to believe any of these claims, though at the same time, there is not reason to doubt the sincerity of their authors. Suffice it to say that every new seeker after the "truth" of Tarot will be starting from scratch, because the mystery of the cards, if knowable, is not yet known.[3]

Even the interpretations of the word "tarot," which also appeared only toward the end of the 16th century, are very different from each other. They are as numerous and imaginative as the stories about the cards' origins. They range from the "royal path" (from Egyptian *tar*—"path" and *ro*—"king") to the divine law (from the Hebrew *Torah*) to the quite profane explanation that a river called the Taro flows close to the northern Italian city of Parma and the cards probably came from this valley. The only thing we know for certain is that tarot is a French word in which the last "t" is not pronounced. Those who insist on pronouncing it anyway want to emphasize that the first and last "t" belong together, almost overlapping each other as if the word were

---

2 Max Luginbuehl, *Das Geheimnis des Dreikraeftespiels* (Pfullingen: Baum, 1961).
3 Cynthia Giles, *The Tarot* (New York: Paragon House, 1992), p. 70.

written in a circle on a wheel, which is one further meaning of the word: *rota* (Latin)— "the wheel." If we also add the Egyptian word *orat* ("announced") and remember that Ator was an Egyptian goddess of initiation, then we can understand the sentence that the American occultist Paul Foster Case has created from the four pronounced letters of the name: ROTA TARO ORAT TORA ATOR = *The wheel of the tarot announces the law of initiation.*

The truth about the origin of the cards and the meaning of the name will certainly lie somewhere in between the various speculations. I personally find the question of the actual age of the cards to be insignificant. If the tarot has been handed down to us as archetypal wisdom rooted in the depths of the collective unconscious, and if it extends back into even earlier history of the dawn of human consciousness, as this book will show, then it is actually irrelevant whether the cards that illustrate this wisdom are 400 or 4,000 years old. In any case, the images that the major arcana convey to us are older than paper and the art of printing.

Only the 22 cards of the major arcana conceal this wisdom in their profound symbolism. The 56 minor arcana have no such dimension. "[T]he fact that no occult or other writer has attempted to assign anything but a divinatory meaning to the minor arcana," justifies for A. E. Waite, "in yet another manner that the two series do not belong to one another."[4] Furthermore, he says that he recognizes once and for all that the major trumps belong to the divine dealings of philosophy and the rest of the cards to fortune-telling. The cards of the minor arcana have never been interpreted into a language that transcends that of fortune-telling.[5]

Up until the beginning of the 20th century, these 56 cards were not illustrated in any way more expressive than that of our playing cards. They showed the number of symbols corresponding to the value of the cards. This means that three cups were seen on the III of Cups and there were nine pentacles on the IX of Pentacles (figure 1, page 6). These cards were just as difficult to interpret as the III of Hearts or the IX of Diamonds. The meanings of all the minor arcana cards had to be learned by heart. The symbolism of the number was combined with the quality of the respective elements[6] and a conclusion was drawn. This changed in 1910, when a new set of tarot cards was designed by A. E. Waite, painted by Pamela Colman Smith, and published by

---

[4] A. E. Waite, *The Pictorial Key to the Tarot* (York Beach, ME: Samuel Weiser, 1973), p. 66.
[5] A. E. Waite, *The Pictorial Key to the Tarot,* pp. 167-168.
[6] Wands—fire, Swords—air, Pentacles—earth, Cups—water.

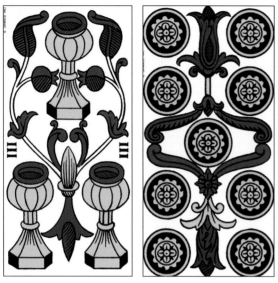

Figure 1. The III of Cups and IX of Pentacles in the traditional depiction.

Figure 2. The same cards in the illustrated Waite Tarot by Arthur Edward Waite and Pamela Colman Smith.

Rider & Co. in London. The minor arcana was illustrated for the first time (figure 2). Since then, pictures lead to the meaning of all 78 cards on many decks that have been created since that time. The Waite deck (often called the Rider-Waite deck) is probably still the most popular tarot deck of all the decks used today.

As welcome as the enrichment may be, we should not miss the great difference between the pictures that have emerged from the collective unconscious of humanity through the course of the centuries (as can be seen from the 22 major arcana cards) and the illustrations that have been thought up by one human being (the minor arcana), no matter how inspired this person may be. A picture is certainly helpful in illustrating a meaning; however, it can never achieve the content and symbolic depth of an archetypal picture. For this reason, it is less productive to ponder about details in the pictures of the minor arcana. The III of Cups shows us the harvest festival, as can be seen in the fruits at the feet of the dancers. Anyone who recognizes this message in the illustration knows what the card wants to say: a development has taken a good course, the harvest has been brought in, and the person is thankful and content. This picture illustrates nothing more. Any speculation about why one of the dancing graces is wearing golden shoes while the other wears blue, or what type of fruits and vegetables are displayed in it are secondary, if not futile.

The 22 major arcana are symbols of a person's path in life. And a symbol is—in contrast to the signs, icons, codes, and ciphers—nothing artificial or invented. A symbol doesn't attempt to conceal anything apparent. To the contrary, it illustrates something that is greater and extends deeper than words can express or that our minds can comprehend. If the circle is the symbol for the original undivided whole, paradise, the divine hemisphere, the unity of all, the unconscious and superconsciousness, the self, completion, eternity, and much more, then these meanings have never been invented. Instead, inherent knowledge has been perceived in the symbol of the circle—and this applies to all cultures of humanity.

The key to the symbols is less likely to be found in the various secret societies, orders, or lodges that call themselves esoteric, and much more in a deep understanding of the human soul. In the 20th century, the Swiss psychologist C. G. Jung has opened up a valuable approach to our understanding of archetypal symbolism, and to what has often been called the secret wisdom, which is still the proper name for it. However, this is neither mystery-mongering nor finding a hidden meaning, and certainly not a conscious obscuring of knowledge with the goal of keeping it secret. The archetypal images are insights that are secret in their nature because they have been gained from the essential, yet invisible, correlations behind the outer world of appearances, from the reality behind the reality. In a conspicuously similar manner, this actually esoteric knowledge is found in all cultures, and is older than any religion. It usually forms the original root of religions; in some cases, it has been preserved as the innermost core of religious philosophy. At its center is the question about an individual's path in life and the meaning of death.

Condensed in the smallest way possible, the thought at the basis of such secret wisdom is that we live in a polarized reality, in a world in which we can only perceive and comprehend something when we can think of an opposite pole as a reference point. It would not occur to us to call (or perceive) something as masculine if there were no

The redesigners of the cards. Arthur Edward Waite [1857–1942] (from the collection of R. A. Gilbert), and Pamela Colman Smith [1878–1951] (From the *Encyclopedia of the Tarot*, vol. III, by Stuart Kaplan © 1990, Stamford, CT: US Games Systems. Reproduced by permission. Further reproduction prohibited).

feminine counterpart. Without night, there would be no day; without death, we wouldn't know we are alive. If we comprehend this law of polarity as the all-encompassing principle of our reality, then we can conclude that there is also an opposite pole to polarity itself—the unimaginable unity that all religions describe in their own way, with their respective images and symbols as divine and paradisiac. The fall from this original unity, the state of conflict, the multiplicity, and the possible return to a lost paradise is the esoteric knowledge about the individual path in life.

This is why all spiritual teachings describe this path as a path of healing because its goal is the wholeness of the human being. Here we assume, as in Jungian psychology, that the starting human situation is "unwhole" insofar as portions of wholeness are initially located in the so-called "shadow," an area that is experienced by the conscious mind as foreign or absent, and an area that can only gradually become conscious. As long as parts of our essential nature lie in the shadows, we are not only missing them in terms of our wholeness, but they are simultaneously the vital source for some types of misguided behavior with which they—in simplified terms—want to draw attention to themselves. This path is made visible in the 22 pictures of the major arcana. This is what makes these cards so unique. They have a dimension that goes far beyond everything that can be read when laying the cards. Here lies the deeper meaning, the actual heart of the tarot. An individual who comprehends these correlations, recognizing them as images on the path in life, will find the major arcana to be a fascinatingly clear assistance in personal orientation.

In addition, the question arises as to whether the original symbolism of these cards is distorted when newly designed tarot cards appear. Some of the new decks published today have completely different motifs, and additions that did not exist on the cards in their previously quite simple state. Modern students of the tarot have to think about whether or not the actual meaning of the card has been understood and enriched by analogous symbols, or if the change is a distortion of the original meaning of the symbol. For example, when a tarot deck shows a Hanged Man who is strung up on the gallows, we can assume that the creator of this card used the original name of the card but doesn't understand its actual meaning. On the other hand, if The Hanged Man is hung on a T-shaped cross with the right (= conscious) instead of the left (= unconscious) leg, the sign of the chosen one (see figure 3), this includes an enrichment of the original symbolism that distorts nothing but goes beyond what previously existed. It makes it clear that the sacrifice involved here could also be voluntarily

Figure 3. The Hanged Man from the Marseilles Tarot; The Hanged Man in the Waite Tarot; and The Hanged Man from the Crowley Tarot.

and consciously made by the chosen one. And if the wood of the cross also sprouts fresh shoots, this is an indication of new vital strength, which has been produced by the sacrifice.

The Hanged Man in the tarot published by Aleister Crowley in 1944 (the Crowley Thoth Tarot Deck) shows a person crucified helplessly between life and death (see figure 3). While the Snake of Life still holds him up—like the proverbial silk thread—his attention (his head) is directed toward the lower Snake of Death. None of this is a falsification of the original symbolism, but rather an amplification, which means an enrichment; a technique that has also proved to be useful in other areas of symbols, such as Jungian dream work, to understand dream symbolism.

There is a change in the Waite Tarot that many people hardly recognize; yet, I am convinced that it distorts the meaning of the deck. Waite renumbered the Justice and Strength cards. Justice was originally in the 8th position and Strength in the 11th, and Waite switched these two cards. In his "corrected" tarot, as he called it, Strength now became the eighth card and Justice received the eleventh position (see figure 4 on page 10).

Since Waite gave no significant reason for this change, there are naturally many speculations about what may have caused him to make it. The Cabala, the Jewish secret teaching, has the tree at its center—

Figure 4. Left column: Justice and Strength with the traditional numbering; middle column: the renumbered cards in the Waite tarot by Arthur Edward Waite and Pamela Colman Smith; right column: the original sequence, but new names (Adjustment and Lust) in the cards by Aleister Crowley.

called the Tree of Life—as a comprehensive symbol of Creation. It consists of ten energy centers, called sephirah in the singular and sephiroth in the plural, which are connected with each other by 22 paths. While the ten sephiroth correspond to the ten cardinal numbers on one level, the 22 paths have their parallels in the 22 letters of the Hebraic alphabet and—as some people presume—in the 22 cards of the major arcana. With this background, Waite appears to have found renumbering the cards necessary. However, in opposition to this perspective, Aleister Crowley, who was just as knowledgable about the Cabala, reinstated the old sequence in his Thoth Tarot.

Another speculation assumes that a few sages consciously changed the structure of the cards in ancient times in order to confuse non-initiates. Even if such a consideration could naturally never by excluded with certainty, almost everything seems to speak against this assumption. For one thing, this confuses the above-described illuminative nature of symbols with a secret language that people have invented to encode a body of knowledge. On the other hand, such an exchange of positions would be so harmless that it would stop no one making a serious effort to crack the "code." As will be shown in the course of this book, on the basis of the mythological background of the cards, the original structure of the cards is far more convincing. We can also come to the same conclusion by comparing the symbolism of the numbers eight and eleven with the respective themes of the cards.

How to Use This Book

LAYING THE TAROT CARDS IN ORDER TO FIND AN ANSWER to a question that has been posed is just one way of approaching the tarot. This book shows another, less known, yet very insightful approach to a profound level of the tarot. It involves using the 22 cards of the major arcana as meaningful signposts—we could even understand them to be archetypal milestones—on the path to a treasure that is hard to find, which is wholeness or individuation. The many cross-connections that result between the individual cards not only allow insightful correlations of meaning to be recognized, but also clearly bring to light an illuminating life philosophy that has been handed down in the tarot. Once we have penetrated and internalized this knowledge, the cards will be more than a valuable help in orientation. We will understand the tasks, experiences, and crises into which life leads us, as well as our experiences of happiness, on a much more comprehensive level and in a greater context of meaning.

If you think you recognize yourself in several of the stages while reading this book, this should not surprise you. On the one hand, the 22 cards of the major arcana represent the entire range of experiences that we encounter on the path in life that is possible for us. The limitation of being "possible for us" means to say that there is no guarantee of reaching the last card. They create a potential. However, the same sequence of cards shows us images of our developmental path in a great variety of areas in life; moreover, each section of the path bears the structure of the whole within itself, in accordance with the Hermetic Law of the "macrocosm equals the microcosm." For example, the result may be that we simultaneously find ourselves at the following stages (tarot cards) in life:

1. At **The Hanged Man** on our path in life, a typical stage that occurs not only in the middle of life.

2. At **The World** in terms of our occupation or profession once we have found our place.

3. Between **The Devil** and **The Tower** in terms of a relationship if we have entangled ourselves in dependencies and want to break out, or—and this experience is also possible at the same stage—when we perceive our own shadow theme (**The Devil**) in the friction and conflicts and repeatedly break out of the old pattern (**The Tower**).

4. At **The Star** in the resolution of personal problems since we have just succeeded in a very decisive breakthrough (**The Tower**), and are once again hopeful and looking for new horizons (**The Star**), but first have to bring this still uncertain and unsecured experience or perception over the threshold (**The Moon**) into the light, into real life (**The Sun**) so that it can create solutions there (**Judgement**) and find its lasting place (**The World**).

5. At The Chariot in the beginning of a new project because we have already recognized our plans to be meaningful (**The Hierophant**) and have decided to take the risk (**The Chariot**) with our whole hearts (**The Lovers**).

6. Involved in "hatching" (**The Empress**) an impulse (**The Magician**), which has triggered an inner process that is still unconscious (**The High Priestess**) and now wants to take form (**The Emperor**).

7. In the area of consciousness development, in a phase of retreat at **The Hermit** when it comes to perceiving our individuality in order to comprehend our task in life (**Wheel of Fortune**) with this knowledge.

Seen in this light, this is an approach to the cards that doesn't require laying them. Instead, the right card results by understanding it to be a reflection of the current situation; in addition, through its surrounding field, it allows correlations to become clear that are helpful for both a deeper understanding and the further orientation in life. Of course, the reverse path is also possible. When we have lost our orientation, we can also draw one card of the major arcana in order to see how the tarot describes our present situation. The keywords at the end of each section give us advice about which tasks are at hand and the risks that should be considered in the process.

THE JOURNEY OF THE HERO

A Parable for the Human Being's Path in Life

*When a myth is enacted in a ritual performance or . . .
when a fairy-tale is told, the healing factor within it acts
upon whoever has taken an interest in it and allowed
himself (or herself) to be moved by it in such a way
that through this participation he (or she) will be
brought into connection with an archetypal form
of the situation and by this means enabled to
put himself (or herself) "into order."*[1]

---

[1] Emma Jung and Marie-Louise von Franz, *The Grail Legend* (New York: Putnam, 1970), p. 37. Material in parentheses is mine.

The journey of the hero is the oldest story in the world. As the basic structure, it is woven into myths, fairy tales, and legends that tell us how a person sets out to accomplish the great work. It is the story behind all these stories, which to this very day are always told in the same way under countless names in all languages and cultures over and over again. No one has ever devised, invented, or thought up this story. Instead, a direct knowledge of the soul is expressed in this story; one could say a knowledge that we have "brought along" with us. As the oldest story in the world, it is also an exemplary story, a parable for the human being's path in life. This is what makes it so interesting, and this is why it must be told time and again so that we never forget why we are on the Earth and what we have to do here.

Origin and Meaning of the Hero's Journey

Many ethnologists, psychologists, philosophers, and sociologists have studied this treasure that is concealed in our myths and fairy tales, researching its roots. Above all, we thank the Swiss depth psychologist C. G. Jung for the illuminating explanation of this phenomenon that the motifs of these traditions are apparently innate in the soul of every human being. He proved that we human beings not only have outer characteristics, on the basis of which each of us can be recognized as a human being, independent of our age, race, and gender. There is also something common on the level of the soul that is characteristic of every human being. Jung called this inner realm the *collective unconscious.* On this level, which connects all human beings, the archetypes of the human soul have their effects. These are the images that are inherent to us, which we virtually find, which we have "brought" with us and do not have to first acquire in life through experience. The wise old man is such an archetype, for example. He could even appear in the dream of a person who has actually never seen or heard of such an old man. Even without an external example, the unconscious mind is capable of showing us an archetypal image from the collective layer. The same also applies to angels, an archetype for which the chances of never having seen it before are considerably greater.

The journey of the hero is the archetypal pattern of a range of actions woven from these primordial images. This is why, despite its many variations, the journey and the image are always so strangely

Figure 5. The world before and after the Copernican turning point. Mother Earth stands at the center of all existence in the geocentric perspective (top). In the heliocentric depiction (bottom), everything revolves around the Sun. (From *Harmonia Macrocosmica*, by Andreas Cellarius, Prussian State Library, Berlin.)

familiar to us. They always tell of the quest, the adventurous search for the treasure that is hard to find, and are composed of elementary components. The philologist Walter Burkert has summarized these components as follows:

An initial loss or mission results in a task, which the hero must accomplish. He sets out on the path, meets adversaries and helpers along the way, wins a decisive magic charm, faces the opponent, overcomes him, and is often marked in the process; he gains what he has sought, sets out on the path home, and shakes off pursuers and competitors. At the end, there is a wedding and accession to the throne.[2]

Yet, as often as this story has been told, as many collections of fairy tales and myths as it may fill, only once has it taken on a complete form as a whole in pictures—and this is in the 22 tarot cards of the major arcana. However, not only are the archetypal events illustrated in these motifs, many connections between individual stages become transparent in the structure of the cards. Their meaning for our path in life becomes comprehensible on the deepest level.

Essential motifs of the hero's journey were apparently read from the heavens. Above all, the movements of the two great lights, the sun and the moon, have served as models. In order to understand this

2 Walter Burkert, *Mythos und Mythologie,* in: *Propyläeen Geschichte der Literatur,* vol. 1 (Berlin: Propyläeen Verlag, 1981), p. 14.

background, we must consider the world in the way that it looked to people throughout the millennia before Galileo and Copernicus brought about the great turning point (see figure 5).

Today we know that Earth rotates on its own axis and around the Sun. However, if we follow our perception, the Sun continues to rise in the morning and set in the evening. Despite all the scientific discoveries of past centuries, nothing has changed in this experience. And if we want to understand the story that the soul tells us, we must open up to its reality and see the world as it has shown itself to humanity since time immemorial.

Heracles' sea journey at night. Heracles in the Sun Beaker (vase, Vatican Museum).

The World Mountain, upon which human beings live, is found at the center. Mighty columns stand at both sides. The left column is crowned by the Moon, the right by the Sun. Together they bear the vault of the heavens, under which we live safe and secure.

This ancient concept becomes even more vivid in the schematic depiction that the Babylonian view of the world shows us (see figure 6 on page 20). Here the World Mountain rises up on the center

Byzantine worldview; the World Mountain with columns that bear the heavens (Vatican Library).

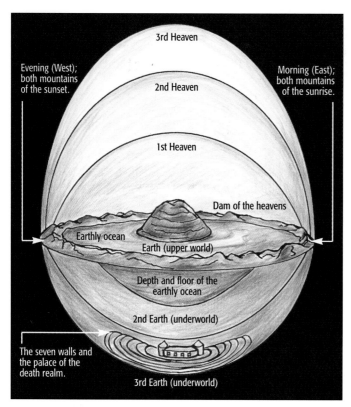

Figure 6. The Babylonian worldview. (Adapted from *Babylonisches Weltbild* by Gerhard J. Bellinger. Knaurs Gruber Religionsführer Munich, 1990, p. 50.)

disk, which is surrounded by an ocean. The ring of the horizon bears the spheres, through which the planets travel; the underworld is found beneath the horizon.

In this Babylonian worldview, it is possible to study two phenomena that human beings have puzzled about since ancient times, and for which they have sought an explanation over and over again. How is it possible that the Sun sets every evening in the west and appears in a wondrous manner the next morning again in the east? How does it get there? No one saw it at night, and yet it is on the other side again every morning. Clever minds have developed various theories. One presumes that the Sun gets on a barque in the evening at the gateway of the west—which is sometimes equated with a reclining crescent Moon—from which it is carried across the night sky. Since the night sky is seen as the night sea, the story of the hero's sea journey at night has arisen from this image of the nighttime sea journey of the Sun.

However, in other places—and these were presumably the coastal areas—the news spread that the Sun actually disappeared behind the horizon every evening; therefore, there must be an underworld that the Sun crosses at night. This motif gave rise to the stories of the descent into the underworld, which tell us about how the souls of the dead thirst for the coming of the light and the vital energy of the Sun, rejoicing as soon as it dips into the realm of the shadows. It also resulted in stories that report how the powers of the light always fight against the powers of darkness at the witching hour; the triumphal rising of the Sun every morning shows new evidence of its continually victorious powers.

An important motif was also read in the movement of the Moon, the second largest light in the heavens. At the end of its cycle, and therefore at the end of the original month, the crescent of the old Moon can been seen for one last time in the morning on the *eastern* horizon. This is followed by an average of three moonless nights before the new light can be seen again for the first time in the *western* sky at sunset in the evening. During the three days and nights in between, the Moon apparently crosses through the underworld since how else could it suddenly appear in the west after it was last seen in the east? Analogous to this heavenly occurrence, there is, in the traditions of many peoples, the story of a hero who descends into the underworld in order to complete a great work there, and who returns victoriously or rises from the dead after three days. We are certain to be familiar with this motif from the Bible and the Christian creed of faith, in which it says that Jesus was: "crucified, died, and buried, descended into Hell, and rose again from the dead on the third day . . ."

The ancient Egyptians, to whom we are grateful for important knowledge about the correlations and symbols of the hero's journey (and therefore the cards of the major arcana) have depicted the journey of their sun god Ra in very rich images. In his barque, which was called the "barque of the million years," he crossed the day and night sky anew each day.

This motif can also be found in the 22 cards of the major arcana: The single-digit cards I to IX tell of the journey of the Sun through the day sky, while the two-digit cards from X to XVIII tell of the descent into the underworld and the return to the light. As a result, each two respective cards linked with each other through the cross sum have corresponding meanings.

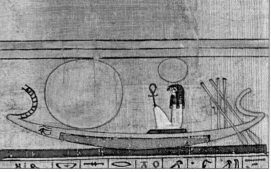

The Egyptian Sun God in the barque of the million years. Left: the journey through the night sea [starry sky]; right: the journey through the day sky [sun disk] (Papyrus of Ani, British Museum, London).

Figure 7. The daily arc of the Sun, and the journey through the underworld, in the pictures of the major arcana.

Figure 8. The goal of the journey.

The turning point of this journey is marked by The Hermit and The Moon. Although the crab (Cancer) can easily be recognized on The Moon card, we must consult astrology in order to know that The Hermit corresponds to Saturn and the sign of Capricorn. This means that these cards also reflect the turning points in the yearly cycle of the Sun, the Tropic of Cancer and the Tropic of Capricorn.

The leitmotifs for both stretches of the path are found in the first two arcana. For the *single*-digit cards, card one states the theme: it is The Magician who shows the masculine path of becoming conscious, which runs from the left (unconscious) to the right (conscious). On the other hand, The High Priestess (II) is the key to the feminine path of the *two*-digit cards, which runs from right to left and describes turning to what is dark, unconscious, and secretive—the path through the mysteries. This naturally is not the path of the male or the path of the female; for in order to become whole, man and woman must take both the masculine and the feminine path. The hero's journey is also the journey of the heroine, even if most of the myths that have been preserved in patriarchal history tend to tell one-sided stories of heroes who accomplish the great work.

The analytical psychologist C. G. Jung describes the growth of the self as the process of individuation, which involves discovering and developing your individual uniqueness and letting your own pattern in life take shape so you can find yourself and ultimately go beyond this to find wholeness. This path—comparable to the path of the sun—can also be subdivided into two sections, whereby the first half of life serves self-development and growth in the external sense. By way of contrast, turning back to the inside world and encountering the shadow are the themes of the second half of life. The goal or the fruit of the path of individuation, the unified personality that has matured to wholeness, is the theme of the last three major arcana cards.

Those who have passed through both worlds reach the themes of these cards, XIX to XXI, at the end. They represent the return to the light—The Sun, the mystery of transformation—Judgement, and paradise regained—The World (see figure 8 on page 23). The 22nd card with the number 0 is The Fool. Shakespeare's clown says of him: "Foolery, sir, does walk about the orb like the sun."[3]

---

[3] Shakespeare, *Twelfth Night*, Act 3, Scene 2.

THE MAJOR ARCANA

Isn't it strange that of all people The Fool should be the hero who succeeds in the great journey? Today we understand heroes to be completely different characters. They are courageous, strong, unwavering, clever, and always surrounded by the aura of the eternal winner. However, if we go back in history, we can see that all these courageous, invincible heroes come from a relatively recent era, even if some of them—like Gilgamech, Heracles, Orion, or Perseus—can even look back on a history of three or four thousand years. This distinctly masculine type of hero is a characterization from the early dawn of patriarchy and is substantially different from his older role models, with which we are just as familiar. They have continued to live in the oral traditions, in our fairy tales and legends. There—at least at the beginning—the hero is never particularly cour-

The Fool
The Hero of the Story

ageous, strong, gallant, or skillful. Far from it, he is always the youngest, the idiot, the fool. But interestingly enough, it is precisely this "simpleton" who succeeds in accomplishing the great work. These stories all have the same basic pattern. For example, they tell of how a shadow falls over a blossoming kingdom and the king lets a hero be sought who is willing to risk his life to save the land from threatening ruin. The king usually has three sons, and the two older sons immediately say they are willing to solve the problem. They are more or less sincere, yet they constantly attempt to complete the tests without success. When the youngest son prepares to try as well, everyone laughs at him and considers him lost. He knows that he isn't particularly smart, courageous, or skillful, but he takes the risk, and sets off on his way. And after many trials and wondrous occurrences, he finds the treasure that is so hard to find, brings it home, and can therefore free the land from the great danger.[1] The king would have believed anyone else capable of this deed, most of all his oldest sons, who very much resemble him and are almost as clever and brave as he is (or was once); but certainly he doesn't believe that his youngest son is going to be the hero.

---

[1] There are naturally many female equivalents for the story in which the youngest daughter, in contrast to her – frequently evil – siblings, is the heroine. For example, Cinderella, Psyche, or King Lear's youngest daughter.

Parzival in fool's clothing; Parzival leaving his mother and his home [detail] (Edmund von Wörndle, Perceval Hall Vinzentium, Brixten).

This is precisely where the remarkable message of the fairy tales of all the people of this world can be found. They tell us that the person who solves the greatest problems is always the only person who we don't think will be able to do it. Marie-Louise von Franz gives us the explanation for this: "The simpleton . . ." so she says, "symbolizes the basic genuineness and integrity of the personality . . . . This integrity is more important than intelligence or self-control, or anything else. It is this genuineness . . . which saves the situation."[2] It would be premature and wrong to draw the conclusion that this is the journey of The Fool. Although the hero begins the journey as The Fool, he grows up very quickly. However, toward the end of the story, he must find his way back to a simple and modest outlook that is similar to his initial attitude. Like Parzival, who went out into the world in fool's clothing and once again found the Castle of the Holy Grail at the end of the story as the pure fool, we also encounter The Fool here as the dumb simpleton at the beginning of the story; he will appear at its completion as the wise Fool.

The card shows The Fool accompanied by a dog, which symbolizes the helpful powers of the instincts that protect The Fool on his path. Although he has no idea that he is standing directly at the abyss, he will not fall into it. The barking of the dog warns him or—what is even more probable—he lets himself be enticed away in another direction without ever learning how close to the abyss he stood. The snow-covered

THE HERMIT.

THE FOOL.

Figure 9. The snow-covered heights on the horizon of The Fool show the world in which The Hermit is at home. They represent the heights of knowledge that The Hermit has attained, but to which The Fool must still climb.

2 Marie-Louise von Franz, *Shadow and Evil in Fairy Tales* (Zurich: Spring, 1974), p. 185.

mountains in the background of the card represent the heights that he still must climb on his journey. These peaks are the home of The Hermit, who embodies the goal of the first half of the path at the end of the single-digit cards. This goal is called knowledge or—better yet—self-knowledge. The Fool carries everything that he takes along on the journey in his bag; there has already been a lot of speculation about its contents (see figure 9 on page 29). Sheldon Kopp found the best explanation. He called it "the wallet of unused knowledge."[3]

This also expresses the typical, but important, basic attitude of The Fool. He either knows nothing, or he doesn't make use of his knowledge. This is why he also is not obstructed or blocked by what he knows. On one level, he personifies the child within us; and we know that children love to try new things time and again, playfully taking unfamiliar paths. Without a doubt, this unbiased openness is the best approach for learning something that is truly new. This is why Waite also called this card "the mind in search of knowledge."

However, the more adult we become, the more we tend to stick to our own notions and repeatedly confirm our opinions. This means that we think we are right all the time, and we are increasingly less interested in how the reality behind our ideas really looks. Instead, we live in a world of concepts that we proudly call our pragmatic knowledge. This attitude blocks our ability to open up to insights. We hold onto our images and judgments because they are familiar and make us feel secure. No wonder that life becomes increasingly boring and turns into a monotonous treadmill—our joy in life sinks beneath the freezing point and there is nothing new and exciting to look forward to. And it is also no wonder that the living reality catches up to us time and again and we—partly through extreme crises—must recognize that we have once again created a false picture for ourselves.

In contrast with this, The Fool stands for the cheerful, uncomplicated side of us that does not care whether something is perfect or whether we make a mistake. Instead, it joyfully tries out new things, without the fear of embarrassment or failure, or of making itself look ridiculous. If something doesn't work out, he tries again until he succeeds or loses interest. He likes to be happy from the bottom of his heart and is astonished by all the possibilities in life and the immense variety that this world offers us.

---

[3] Sheldon B. Kopp, *The Hanged Man* (Palo Alto, CA: Science and Behavior Books, 1974), p. 7.

Keywords for THE FOOL

ARCHETYPE:	The child, the naive simpleton
TASK:	Trying out new things without any bias, playful learning
GOAL:	Joy in life, playfully gathering experiences
RISK:	Awkwardness, confusion, carelessness, foolishness
FEELING IN LIFE:	Adventurousness, curiosity, sure instincts, astonished openness, carefree joy, curiosity, the desire to try things out

THE MAGICIAN.

THE HIGH PRIESTESS

t is typical for the classic hero to have two sets of parents—a heavenly and an earthly pair. We are familiar with this picture from many myths in which the heroes were children of mighty gods but raised by earthly parents—at something like a royal court. Sometimes this situation is also concealed in the motif of the hero's unknown origin. Fairy tales often give an indication of the "other parents" in that their heroes frequently grow up with stepparents. In the tarot, these doubled parents are shown in the first four numbered cards.

The Magician and The High Priestess represent the heavenly parents of the hero and personify the original polarity of masculine and feminine on the heavenly level, which means "in the world of ideas." Whenever the terms "masculine" and "feminine" are discussed in this book, they mean neither a division of roles nor the sum of all masculine or feminine qualities, but solely the

The Magician and The High Priestess
The Heavenly Parents

symbolic meaning of these terms. The archetypal masculine, along with the archetype of the feminine, is an expression of the two original principles that—like yin and yang—can only form the whole together. They symbolize both poles of the duality with which our consciousness perceives reality. For a list of masculine and feminine words, see page 34.

The same duality also manifests itself in the two paths that lead us to knowledge—the magical and the mystical paths. In turn, these paths correspond with the two fundamental possibilities of encountering nature: to intervene or to adapt.[1] The path of The Magician is taken by the Faustian individual who—in search of knowledge—explores and penetrates nature, wanting to elicit its secrets in order to understand and ultimately rule over it. Above all, this is the path taken by the Western human being, and it has produced our current living standard, along with the blessing and curse of technology. It is the active path of external power and action, through which "everything possible" is done; if things go wrong or are experienced as disturbing, then it is just

---

[1] Incidentally, these are also the two possibilities for understanding Darwin's theory of "survival of the fittest," which is normally translated as the "survival of the strongest." But "to fit" also means "to adapt," so the phrase also means "survival of the best-adapted."

MASCULINE	FEMININE	MASCULINE	FEMININE
Active	Passive	Logos	Eros
Right	Left	Causal	Analogous
Above	Below	Abstract	Concrete
Day	Night	Analysis	Synthesis
Sun	Moon	Detailed	Holistic
Flow	Ebb	Separate	Connect
Conscious	Unconscious	Distance	Closeness
Mind	Soul	Outside	Inside
Reason	Intuition	Direct	Indirect
Quantity	Quality	Extensive	Intensive
To have	To be	Extreme	Moderate
Penetrating	Permeable	Linear	Cyclical
Taking action	Letting things happen	Angular	Round
		Hard	Soft
Engendering	Conceiving	Harsh	Mild
Tension	Relaxation	Justice	Morality
Renewing	Preserving	Law	Mercy
Acting	Reacting	Light	Dark
Extroverted	Introverted	Major key	Minor key
Voluntary	Involuntary	Constant	Changeable
Concept	Picture	Uncover	Conceal

as possible to get rid of them again. In both cases, the energy of The Magician is correspondingly directed toward active behavior, in contrast to the High Priestess who shows the path of the mystical human being and represents the art of "being able to let things happen." This is the view of life that we are most likely to find reflected in the Eastern traditions. Taking this mystical path means being ready, while practicing patience, until we are found, touched, and transformed by the divine. In more simplified terms—The Magician seeks, the mystic lets herself be found. Both are paths of knowledge that find their analogies in the polarity of Creation, as well as in the two halves of our brains. Neither path is more important, correct, or better than the other. Each path is bad when exaggerated, but valuable and good when it is taken to the right degree. The hero of our story will—like each of us—have to take both paths in turn to reach the goal.

The Magician: The Heavenly Father

THE MAGICIAN.

THE MAGICIAN PERSONIFIES THE ACTIVE, creative principle. He stands for the solar consciousness that illuminates all things and strives for transparency and clarity. The card shows him in the pose of the master who does not act on the basis of his own strength, but receives his energy from above and makes it effective on Earth. This connection between above and below is also expressed in the wand and the infinity sign (lemniscate). It symbolizes the connection of two worlds and their constant, alternating exchange.

The square table in front of The Magician represents—corresponding with the number four—the level of earthly reality. The symbols lying on it are those of the four tarot suits—Wand and Sword, Cup and Pentacle—as representatives of the four elements—fire and air, water and earth. In their entirety, they also embody wholeness since, according to the ancient Graeco-Roman teachings, the entire Creation has been formed from these four elements. They lie here as tasks, in more precise terms, as the task in life to be mastered by The Magician. Therefore, this card represents intelligence and skill, as well as the will and the power to master the tasks that are given to us in life in order to become whole through them.

The fact that The Magician is not a charlatan, but a valuable force directed at the highest goal, is attested to by the red roses (divine love), the white lilies (purity of the soul), as well as the card's golden background, which stands for "noble" themes in the major arcana of the Waite Tarot.

Keywords for THE MAGICIAN

ARCHETYPE:	The creator, the master
TASK:	Activity, taking the initiative, giving impulses, facing tasks and mastering them
GOAL:	Mastery, self-fulfillment, perception
RISK:	Megalomania, fantasies of omnipotence, charlatanry
FEELING IN LIFE:	Self-assurance, being connected with great energy reserves

The High Priestess:
The Heavenly Mother

THE HIGH PRIESTESS

AS AN OPPOSITE POLE TO THE MAGICIAN, The High Priestess embodies the passive, receptive principle. She represents the patient willingness to let oneself be guided and wait for the right moment to react to an impulse. She knows that everything has its time; she likes to let things happen without prematurely intervening in their course. So this card is an expression of trust in our inner voice that shows us a specific path and reliably tells us time and again whether we should take action and when, where, and how this should be done.

The High Priestess sits between two columns, each with an upward opening, as symbols of her receptive willingness. They bear the letters B and J, which refer back to the Biblical story of the first temple in Jerusalem. King Solomon had two columns built in front of it called Boas and Jachin (2nd Chronicles 3:17 and 1st Kings 7:21). The original meaning of these columns and their names is unknown, although there has been much speculation about them. Above all, these two columns have found a firm place in the symbolism of Freemasonry. They are black and white on the tarot card, therefore symbolizing the original polarity, such as that between light and dark, day and night, summer and winter, conscious and unconscious. The High Priestess has her throne at the center of this polarity because both sides mean equally as much to her. She doesn't separate and evaluate, but knows that only both poles together can result in the whole. Anyone who splits them into opposites loses not only the original unity, but will also find increasing one-sidedness instead of clarity.

With this background, it would be logical to also read the letters B and J as Baal and Jahweh (Jehovah). Baal was the spouse of Astarte, the mighty Canannite Queen of Heaven, whose cult was a Moon—and therefore a night—cult. Jahweh (Jehovah), the Old Testament God, was worshipped as a god of light[1] who—like all patriarchal deities—preferred to fight the powers of darkness.

---

[1] The following limitation should be "officially" added to this statement since, to the great disaffection of the priests, large portions of the people of Israel even considered Astarte, the Queen of Heaven, to be Jahweh's spouse.

Both forces appear to be of equal value since on the deepest (and simultaneously the highest) level, all hostile separations into light and dark, good and evil, God and Devil, life and death are wrong because they are unrealistic. In our innermost heart we know the wholeness that can only be achieved when light and dark celebrate their marriage beyond all limitations and valuations. This insight, this deep knowledge about the all-encompassing unity is the "wisdom of the womb," embodied by the High Priestess and expressed by the Torah scroll,[2] the divine law, lying in her lap. She does not believe in the letter of the law, but senses the true meaning behind everything that has been said, like Mary, of whom the Christmas story so wonderfully reports: "Mary remembered all these things and thought deeply about them" (Luke 2:19).

The same concept is also expressed by her crown, in which the three phases of the Moon—waxing (☽), full (○), and waning (☾)—are shown, thereby emphasizing the lunar consciousness in addition to cyclical nature. This is what the card represents. It is the indirect light of the Moon that lets us perceive things, even though this may not be with the same clarity and distinctness as the Sun's light. Yet, it makes it possible for us to have insights in the dark areas that always elude the solar consciousness since they disappear when the Sun emerges. The High Priestess therefore stands for the dream worlds, for feeling and sensing, and for intuiting the correlations. She is the source of deepest inspiration, which bubbles with increasing liveliness the more our daytime consciousness descends to a type of "twilight state."

---

[2] The Torah (Tora) is understood to be the five books of Moses, the beginning of the Old Testament. These books contain the law of the Jewish people, which is why the Torah is often equated with the divine law. Originally—and up to this day in the synagogues—these "books" were written on a scroll, which is why the Torah scroll can be seen on the card.

Keywords for THE HIGH PRIESTESS

ARCHETYPE: The Queen of Heaven

TASK: Patiently waiting for an (inner or outer) impulse, waiting for the right moment, being receptive, serving as an echo, being ready

GOAL: Intuitive certainty, deepest understanding, sensing correlations, comprehending dreams, having premonitions of developments

RISK: Fleeing reality, hesitation, continuing indecisiveness

FEELING IN LIFE: Being able to let things happen, trust in being guided, being inspired in a state of reduced consciousness

THE EMPRESS.

THE EMPEROR.

f the heavenly parents show the archetypal masculine and the archetypal feminine in the world of ideas, the earthly parents embody these archetypal principles on the concrete level: as Mother Nature (The Empress) and the force of culture and civilization (The Emperor). If both forces are in harmony with each other, the human being lives in a protected, secure, and positive environment. While Mother Nature, as the source of all life, constantly lets new fruits grow, The Emperor brings in the harvest. Where Mother Nature shows herself in her original wildness, The Emperor knows how to plant gardens in the middle of the wilderness and build protective spaces where people feel safe from the encroachments and moods of nature. Otherwise, nature causes trouble for humans in the form of cold, heat, wet, or storms. While Mother Nature is the quintessence of cyclical changes, The Emperor constantly attempts to balance

The Empress and The Emperor
The Earthly Parents

and regulate these fluctuations as much as possible. Mother Nature may produce the most luscious fruits for many years, but at other times will suddenly let her children starve. This is why he builds grain silos and refrigerators in order to balance these fluctuations, just as he builds heaters and air conditioners to compensate for "her" temperature variations.

Done to a healthy extent, The Emperor's striving is true civilization, which means the refinement of the raw, elemental wildness of nature. However, the extremes of The Emperor's strength leads to flattening out all the cycles, to straightening all the rivers, to concrete jungles and asphalt excesses, monotonous parks, square forests, and the sterile wasteland of an artificial, plastic world. When his structures become too rigid, Mother Nature knows how to soften things or break them up. She lovingly covers ugly concrete walls with ivy and lavishly carpets fields of ruin with flowers. Whatever he creates will rust, go to seed, and fall back to her as soon as he no longer takes proper care of it.

As Mother Nature, The Empress embodies everything natural; on the other hand, The Emperor represents everything created by human hands. She stands for what is round, since a straight line is the exception in her world. He represents everything straight, since he prefers to produce smooth and square things with his hands or his machines. Even her experience of time is round and cyclic, without a beginning and end, and without any actual innovations. It is the course of the year, the eternal return of what has already been here. By way of contrast, his time is linear. Within it, everything has a beginning and an end—and he gives the name of progress to the development in between. This is why it is common knowledge in her world that everything that passes also arises again, accompanied by the belief in the eternal wheel of rebirths. On the other hand, it is known with the same certainty in his linear world that everything has a beginning and an end, therefore concluding that we also only live once.

The Empress:
The Earthly Mother

MOTHER NATURE SITS ON HER THRONE, adorned and surrounded by the symbols of her fertility—the pomegranate on her garment, the grain field, the forest, the river—all show that she is the fertile ground, the source from which all life arises. The twelve jewels in her crown represent the twelve months of the year and identify her as the ruler of the seasons. The Venus sign on her throne emphasizes the peaceful aspect of Mother Nature, her caring, nurturing, and fertile side. Her wild, destructive character, which she can show in the form of natural catastrophes, therefore shifts to the background of the card.

The Empress is the absolute card of creativity and the life force, the almost inexhaustible original source that gives birth to something new over and over again. She represents the fertile phases, living developments, and acts of cyclical renewals.

Keywords for THE EMPRESS

ARCHETYPE:	The mother (Mother Nature)
TASK:	Being fertile, bringing something new into the world
GOAL:	Life force and growth, cyclical renewal, affirmation of life
RISK:	Wild growth, instability
FEELING IN LIFE:	Walking on fertile ground, feeling alive, knowing about the cycles, trust in the abundance

The Emperor:
The Earthly Father

THE EMPEROR PERSONIFIES STRUCTURE, order, clarity, and reality. As a patriarch, he is both the guarantee of security and order, as well as the bearer of great responsibility. His outstanding strength lies in his perseverance and the ability to not lose hold of the red thread. With the general dismantling of the father image in the 20th century, many people find the values that he embodies to be long outdated. Yet, they too quickly forget that he just personifies the power that allows ideas, desires, and intentions to become reality. He is the doer, the effector who knows how to do a proper job. And for all that, he is not hostile to life, of which he has often been unjustly accused. To the contrary: in his right hand he holds the ankh as a scepter, the ancient Egyptian cross with a loop, symbolizing the living connection of the feminine and the masculine with its circle and staff. For the Egyptians, it was purely and simply the symbol of life. This scepter identifies him as a force protecting and maintaining life.

THE EMPEROR.

Keywords for THE EMPEROR

ARCHETYPE: The father (Uncle Sam)

TASK: Uncompromisingly turning ideas, intentions, and perhaps long-held desires into reality

GOAL: Creating order and a secure environment, structure, staying power

RISK: Stubbornness, perfectionism, hardening, rigidity

FEELING IN LIFE: Awareness of responsibility, holding onto the red thread, realistic attitude, and soberness

Heavenly and Earthly Parents

THROUGH THE SEQUENCE OF THE PARENTAL PAIRS (shown in figure 10), the cards already make a fundamental statement about the themes and sections of the hero's journey.

Both pairs of parents appear in the following sequence in the first four cards: masculine (I), feminine (II), feminine (III), and masculine (IV). Since uneven numbers are considered masculine and even numbers are seen as feminine, in a certain way it would make more sense if The Emperor were number III and The Empress were number IV. But there are important messages in this peculiar structure of these cards:

1. The earthly level is a mirror image of the heavenly realm, which is why the earthly parents appear inverted—as in a mirror.

2. Everything that becomes tangible and takes form in this world is subject to the rhythm of four. For this to occur, it requires a procre-

Figure 10. Heavenly and Earthly Parents.

ative impulse (I) that meets with a positive echo, a willingness to receive (II). The impulse will remain ineffective without an echo. Without the impulse, there is no echo. But, once the two have found each other—the one and two unite to form the three—then the fruit can mature (III), which ultimately takes on its own, concrete form (IV). On the level of becoming a human being, these steps correspond with the following: the sperm (I), the egg (II), the fetus (III), and the moment in which the child sees the light of the world and its form becomes visible (IV). In a creative process, these steps are: the idea (I), the positive resonance, the fertile ground that it needs in order to not ineffectively go to waste (II), the maturing of the project (III), and its concrete translation into reality (IV).

3. This structure also makes an important statement about the hero's journey. These first four cards already show what the journey is about and which tasks must be accomplished on which stretch of the path. The masculine path is the path of the will, the path of becoming conscious; but it is also the path of the law since it is important to explore and learn the laws of life and the world here. It runs through the single-digit cards and stands under the rulership of card I, The Magician.

In keeping with the quality of this card, it is an active path in which challenges are waiting to be sought, overcome, and mastered. On one level of meaning, this section of the path represents the first half of life. While the hero—and this is each of us—takes this path, it is important for him to separate himself from the mother's womb (III—The Empress), go out into the world and become an adult. Then, around the middle of life, the portents change. Now it is The High Priestess (II) who takes the lead on the feminine path through the two-digit numbers, which leads downward or inward into the mysterious depths of the unconscious mind into the mysteries of life. The lesson to be learned on this path is the art of "being able to let things happen."

The tasks that must now be faced cannot be overcome with even the cleverest tricks. Now it is time to truly become involved, since whatever is left lying on this path can no longer be solved through contemplation or smart phrases, but only by getting involved in these experiences without any reservations. It is the path of the desires and the path of mercy, upon which we do not advance any further when *we* want to, but when *it* wants us to. This path requires the unconditional willingness to let ourselves be led.

So if the first half concerned leaving the mother's womb (III—The Empress) and growing up, the challenge is now to once again become humble and return the masculine symbols of power (IV—The Emperor) that we have acquired and trust a higher power to guide us. The myth researcher and Jungian Joseph Campbell says of this process: "The normal symbols of our desires and fears become converted, in this afternoon of the biography, into their opposites: for it is then no longer life but death that is the challenge. What is difficult to leave, then, is not the womb but the phallus."[1] However, the strength of the ego must be adequately stabilized for these tasks, which is why these two sections of the path cannot be taken in the opposite order. A strong development and stabilization of the ego, an exploration of the laws of life on the path of the Magician, the first half of the path, is required before the path of The High Priestess can be taken. This second path represents the path of the mystic person, the path of grace, which leads to overcoming the ego and moving beyond it back to wholeness.

---

[1] Joseph Campbell, *The Hero with a Thousand Faces* (New York: Pantheon, 1949), p. 12.

THE HIEROPHANT

ierophant was the name given to high priests in the mysteries of classical antiquity. The word has a Greek origin and means "one who teaches the holy things" (*hieros* = "holy," *phantes* = "teach"). In other tarot decks, the card is also simply called The High Priest or—at least in the older sets of cards—The Pope. The two keys at the foot of the throne refer to Peter, the first pope, to whom Jesus said, according to the Biblical tradition: "And I will give you the keys of the Kingdom of Heaven" (Matthew 16:19). Because of this power of the keys, Peter became the gatekeeper at Heaven's door in popular belief, and the two keys became the main symbols in the popes' coat of arms. The three-fold crown, the three crosses on the border of the garment, and the triple crosses of The High Priest are the

The Hierophant
The Education of the Hero

symbols of his responsibility for the three levels of body, soul, and mind, or even Heaven, Earth, and Hell.

In contrast to the previous pictures, in addition to the oversized, archetypal main figure, other people in human form appear for the first time on this card. These are the novices who stand or kneel at the foot of the throne in order to receive instruction from The High Priest. In this motif, there are parallels to the awakening consciousness of the child, the first conscious perception of another person, and looking up to the parents or other adults, who are experienced as oversized. It is the time in which the child gradually awakens from the initial feeling of unity, the connectedness with everything and everyone, in which it begins to say "I" for the first time and increasingly recognizes the difference and the boundary between itself and the others.

The Hierophant finds his correlation in the education of the hero, the essential preparation for what he will later encounter in the world outside. The card stands for the time when his conscience takes shape, when he learns to differentiate good from evil. It also represents trust in God, which the hero will need on his journey and which develops during his childhood.

However, the heart of the instruction is shown by the blessing hand of The High Priest: the extended fingers stand for the visible

Chiron as the teacher of Achilles [detail] (Jean-Baptiste Regnawlt, Louvre, Paris).

The Archer (Sagittarius)
as a centaur (*Tractatus sphaere*,
Bibliotèque Nationale, Paris).

world (what is apparent), while the two bent fingers represent the invisible (what is concealed and transcendent). In numerological mysticism, five, the sum of the fingers, symbolizes the meaning, that which is essential, as can be easily recognized in the word quintessence (Latin *quint* = "five," *essentia* = "nature"). The message is therefore: only those who direct their attention to both can grasp what is essential, the meaning. Those who only look at the outside will find the direction and what is essential in life as little as those who only yearn for the transcendental. This is why the hero must pass through both worlds in order to find the essential things: the outer, conscious world that corresponds to the daily arc of the sun and the inner, unconscious world that corresponds to its night sea journey.

The Nibelungs tell of how Siegfried was raised by the dwarf Regin. In the Greek myths, it was primarily the wise centaur Chiron who was revered as a great teacher and educator. He imparted knowledge and skills to many heroes, like Jason, Ascelpius, Achilles, and Heracles, for their later paths in life. A centaur is often the motif of the zodiac sign of Sagittarius, which in turn corresponds to The High Priest as an archetype.

Keywords for THE HIEROPHANT

ARCHETYPE:	The saint
TASK:	Paying attention to and respecting what is apparent and what is concealed, the search for meaning
GOAL:	The quintessence, the meaning, finding the direction
RISK:	Hypocrisy, condescending attitude, "guru" affectations
FEELING IN LIFE:	Being "supported" by trust in God, experiencing meaningful things

THE LOVERS.

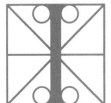 n the Waite Tarot, and in many of the more modern card decks, The Lovers card depicts the theme of pure love. It shows Adam and Eve before the Fall, naked and innocent in Paradise beneath the blessing Raphael, the archangel of lovers. The Tree of Life and the apple-bearing Tree of Knowledge, around which a snake winds, grow behind the two of them. The mountain in the background symbolizes peak experiences, climaxes, and the highest experiences of happiness. If we consider the path of the hero as an analogy to the journey of the sun, with this card we find ourselves at the pinnacle of the course of the sun, its position at noon, and at the same time, the most wonderful experience on the path of becoming conscious.

The Lovers
The Decision

As we will see in its opposite pole of midnight, the card The Devil, there were good reasons for the new design of the card. However, in order to understand what this stage on the hero's journey means, it is necessary to bring to mind the motif of the older tarot cards: it shows us a young man who stands between his mother and his beloved. Above him floats a Cupid holding a bow, whose arrow will very soon hit the youth. Inflamed in this way, with a fiery heart he will decide to leave the parental home—his mother—in order to go his own way (symbolized by the beloved) from now on. However, this image should not be taken too literally, since he obviously has not yet won the heart of his beloved at this point. Perhaps he has seen her briefly one time, or he has heard of her, and now he wants to rescue, conquer, or free her, or whatever he must do. In Mozart's *Magic Flute*, this is the moment in which Tamino first learns from Mother Night that her beautiful daughter Pamina is in the hands of the presumably sinister Sarastros, whereby the young man passionately swears that he will free her. This clear decision made from one's own free will and from the bottom of one's heart is certainly among the most intense experiences of happiness on the path to becoming conscious. The associated determination and resolution is not only the theme of this card, but also the prerequisite for any hero's journey. Without the decision to leave the parental home, the journey would never even take place.

The Lover from the Tarot of Marseilles.

The decision at the beginning of Heracles' path; Heracles at the crossroads (Lucas Cranach, the Elder, Herzog Anton-Ulrich Museum, Braunschweig).

The motif of the older tarot cards was popular in painting, where it significantly enough was called "The Decision" or "The Crossroads." Christianized, it became the symbol of the decision between virtue and vice. Lucas Cranach, for example, has depicted it as such at the beginning of his Heracles cycle.

Keywords for THE LOVERS

ARCHETYPE:	The crossroads
TASK:	Making a decision of one's own free will and from the bottom of one's heart
GOAL:	Declaring intense heartfelt loyalty to one path, one person, one task
RISK:	Effusiveness, gushing enthusiasm
FEELING IN LIFE:	Feeling how the heart is thrilled, determined resolution

ith quick resolve, the hero has climbed into his chariot in order to go out into the world and experience it. Behind him he leaves the city of his childhood, which has given him protection and a sense of security up to now. He holds a staff in his right hand, the golden tip of which represents the noble goals that he is now reaching for—the raising of the treasure, the freeing of the beautiful prisoner, the search for the herb of life, or the lost paradise.

The hero is depicted as the God of Spring, whom people love and have worshipped as the savior, because he brings the warm, fertile seasons and frees them from the cold, the darkness, and the deprivation of the winter. In the entire West, this young, handsome god is considered to be the Queen of Heaven's

The Chariot
The Departure of the Hero

son.[1] Her garment is the starry heavens, which covers the chariot as the canopy on the card; her belt is the zodiac, which she has given her son. As shoulder epaulets, he wears the two moon masks, attributes of the Queen of Heaven, who was also worshipped as the Moon Goddess. Waite called these masks Urim and Thummin, oracle instruments of the high priests of ancient Israel that are mentioned in a number of places (Exodus 28:30, Deuteronomy 33:8, and Ezra 2:63) in the Old Testament, but without any further explanation.[2] Presumably, these were oracle masks, remnants of rites from the cult of the Great Goddess of ancient times.

Just like the hero wears a star on his forehead in some fairy tales, the crown of the charioteer is adorned with an octagonal star that—like the number eight—symbolizes the connection with higher things. On the other hand, the square on his chest—corresponding with the number four—represents earthly reality. This also identifies him as the savior who comes from Heaven (eight) to Earth (four) to accomplish his great work. We are most familiar with this motif, handed down by

---

[1] As, for example, Atis, son of the Phrygian Cybele; Adonis, son of the Greek Aphrodite; Dumuzi, son of the Sumerian Inanna; Tammuz, son of the Babylonian Ishtar; and Baldur, son of the Germanic Frigg.
[2] Urim and Thummin were translated by Martin Luther to mean "light" and "law." More recent translations leave the Hebrew names and interpret them as oracle instruments.

Figure 11. The Tao.

many myths, as it takes form in Jesus Christ, who as the son of the heavenly virgin came to human beings on Earth to redeem them.

A white and a black Sphinx draw the chariot of the hero; each of these also contains the color of the other within itself. The two draft animals therefore take on the symbolism of the Tao, the Chinese symbol of wholeness (see figure 11).

Black and white represent the duality with which our conscious mind perceives reality. Whether the reality actually is like this cannot be said with certainty. We only know that our consciousness is incapable of perceiving or comprehending anything for which it cannot think of an opposite pole as a reference point. We would not recognize masculine to be masculine if there was no feminine; there would be no relaxation without tension; without an image of the Devil, we could not imagine God to be the sum of everything good; and if there was no death, we would not know that we are alive. In this light, life only becomes meaningful and we can only experience it as a result of the fact that we must die.

Although we were born into this duality, we were not aware of it as children. Only with the increasing development of the personality does this fundamental phenomenon become increasingly clear to us. In fact, the words "personality development" quite aptly illustrate what is involved here: the development of what is inherent to us. Figuratively speaking, in the unconscious mind, all of our possibilities are innately "simple" (which means undeveloped and undifferentiated). To develop means to become conscious of our possibilities by raising them out of their unconscious simplicity and unfolding them in our polarized consciousness in order to recognize them. With each of these steps of perception, we understand the outer reality, as well as our inner potential, in a better and more differentiated manner. We become increasingly aware of the tension of opposites within which we live. Between these poles there is naturally a constant field of tension, just as the energy in a magnet attracts or repels. Often enough, we experience friction with this tension and are torn back and forth between the two possibilities offered by the polarity. We take sides within this conflict and endeavor to achieve clarity by judging the one pole to be good and right and the other as bad and wrong, having a high regard of and desire for the one and fearing and rejecting the other. However, the deeper we penetrate within this process, the more often we must perceive that we are not doing justice to the truth with it; the truth is much too complex to be reduced to such a clear formula.

Whenever we are certain that we have found a clear truth, we can simultaneously be sure that it is not *the* truth. Furthermore, the belief in possessing an absolute truth leads every human being into the danger of sooner or later becoming a tyrant who wants to convert others to his supposedly exclusively correct view of the world by any means possible, even through blackmail. This can easily be recognized in the missionary zeal of sectarians—particularly those who have been newly converted—and is unfortunately found much too frequently in esoteric circles as well. This situation can be discovered often enough in the history of the Church, and naturally also on the political stage, where it has already happened more than once that a utopian humanitarian has become a zealous and people-slaughtering despot. Clarity ultimately always means one-sidedness and is therefore the opposite of unity, which always includes both counterpoles. This is why the "Tao te Ching" says:

> The Tao that can be expressed
> is not the eternal Tao;
> the name that can be defined
> is not the unchanging name.[3]

Knowing that our reality is never the absolute reality is not only the basis for true tolerance; above all, it is the basis for the possibility of growing beyond the limits of our previous mental boundary through interested participation in the reality of others, thereby pressing forward to an increasingly deep understanding.[4] Perhaps it will also help us to occasionally remember that not even the colors that we believe we perceive with such certainty are real. There are no colors "out there" but only electromagnetic vibrations that only become colors by means of the observer's eyes and brain. This makes them a highly subjective experience that various people see in quite different ways as their reality.

A unification of opposites is the actual task on the path of development, the goal of which is wholeness and the unity of all things on a higher level. However, this changes nothing about the way we are

---

[3] Lao Tzu, *Tao te Ching*, Ch'u Ta-kao, trans. (London: Allen & Unwin, 1917).
[4] This is precisely the theme of the beautiful story "The King and the Corpse," which Heinrich Zimmer tells in his book *The King and the Corpse: Tales of the Soul's Conquest of Evil*. Joseph Campbell, ed. (New York: Pantheon, 1948).

initially involved with opposites over wide stretches of the path—and it must be this way. In the search for knowledge, we learn to differentiate with increasing preciseness, and we form increasingly fine pairs of opposites, and we usually differentiate between them in a judgmental manner. The result of this development is that an intact world grows with everything that we hold in high esteem, that we love and consider worth striving for; however, another world, full of evil, also grows, which we think should not exist at all. As arrogant as this attitude may seem, it actually assumes that some things went wrong during Creation—and, despite our obviously limited minds, we are allowed the right to have such an opinion. This opinion is indispensable for the necessary development and solidification of our ego consciousness. Without clear borders, a strong ego cannot develop. Without experiencing new differences time and again, the conscious mind remains undifferentiated. Only when we have penetrated the world of opposites deeply enough can and should we practice the art of its unification. We must first create boundaries in order to adequately separate ourselves from everything that we are not[5] so that a strengthened ego can begin to overcome these boundaries.

So The Chariot means that the paradise of childhood, the (unconsciously) experienced unity, is over with the resolute decision of the previous stage (The Lovers). The hero or heroine has entered the polarized world in which his or her consciousness develops, which will allow him or her to awaken. In the process, he or she must avoid becoming torn between the possibilities—the two different draft animals—but also must master the contradictions with skill and unite even opposing forces into a great leap forward. The hero/heroine is still at the beginning. He or she is still inexperienced and well-advised to not overestimate his or her ability since he or she could quickly experience what happened to the sorcerer's apprentice . . .

In the legend of the Grail, this stage corresponds with the moment in which Parzival puts on the armor of the Red Knight, an opponent he has conquered, and thereby—at least externally—changes from a child into a man. Now he looks completely like a knight, the symbol of the higher, more mature human being. However, he still continues to wear his fool's clothing beneath the armor. In order to do justice to the external impression, he will still have to grow on the inside.

---

5 On a very elementary level, this means we are able to clearly say "no" whenever we mean "no."

On the other hand, there are other myths describing the dangers of this stage in which they report of sons of gods falling to Earth. The most prominent examples are Icarus and Phaeton, who fail because they overestimate their unpracticed powers.

As an orientation on this journey, the maps of the soul—as we are familiar with them today as meditation pictures from Tibetan Buddhism in the form of mandalas—can help us. A typical basic structure of these figures consists of a central circle that encompasses a symbol of perfection, such as a Buddha, a Bodhisattva, a depiction of Krishna, an abstract figure, or, in the Western forms—such as the mandalas of St. Hildegard of Bingen—a Christ symbol. This inner circle is surrounded by a cross or a square, which in turn is bordered by an outer circle.

In symbolism, the circle always represents the undivided whole, what is original, or, expressed in graphic terms, paradise. But the cross or the square corresponds to—just as the associated number four—the earthly hemisphere, the world of time

The Sun, an illustration from the tarot by the Master from Ferrara in Italy.

and space. Seen in this way, the mandala with the inner and the outer circle shows us two paradises, between which the cross of time and space lies. These three areas can be illustrated on a great variety of correlative levels. In the language of the fairy tale, the inner circle is the initial paradise, which frequently corresponds with the world of childhood and usually is lost right at the beginning of the story when, for example, the golden ball—the symbol of original wholeness— falls into the fountain.

Mandala. A map for the path of life (Tibetan Thanka, c. 1800 from Philip Rawson's *Tantra: The Indian Cult of Ectasy*, New York and London: Thames and Hudson, 1973).

The cross stands for the world through which we wander in search of the lost paradise, while the outer circle symbolizes the goal, a paradise that corresponds to that of childhood; yet, it is different. The outer and inner circles are similar to each other and have the same center point, but they are not the same. The inner circle is the paradise of ignorance; the other circle is the much more comprehensive paradise of omniscience. In between lies the knowledge of consciousness limited by time and space. Seen in psychological terms, the inner circle symbolizes the unconscious mind, the cross the conscious mind, and the outer circle the superconsciousness. Or, expressed in the terms of C. G. Jung: the unconscious, the ego, and the self. Buddhism calls these three levels unity, separation (multiplicity), and wholeness. The related states are lacking in ego, ego-bound, and free of ego or ignorant, knowing, and wise.

In the legend of the Grail, the Fall is in the background, the expulsion from the Tree of Knowledge, which is always an apple tree in popular belief. In order to find salvation, the knights go on the quest, the search for the Grail, which is said to be found at the Castle of the Holy Grail, sought on the apple-blossom island of Avalon, according to one tradition. In all these cases, it can be seen how the origin and the goal are similar to each other and yet are still not the same because the outer circle, even though it is anchored in the same center, always symbolizes a higher level of development. Seen in this light, the right path in life does not lead to a regression, to sinking into the unconscious mind, but to a breakthrough to something larger, to superconsciousness.

Just as humanity has been able to differentiate between good and evil since eating the fruit from the Tree of Knowledge, the conscience within each of us also awakens with the emerging consciousness. This allows us to perceive what is good and evil. As a result, as the Bible reports, paradise is lost, the paradise of the unity of all things, the lack of differentiation in which there are no values and no tensions of opposites that are so exhausting for human beings. Since then, so it says, we live in sin. This word is also translated as "separation," which corresponds to leaving the inner circle and the loss of the center. Since every person who has become aware of his or her own self has figuratively eaten from the Tree of Knowledge, we have all separated ourselves from the center; this is an inevitable heritage that the Church calls "original sin."

In the major arcana, this theme first appears with the card The Hierophant (The High Priest) since it corresponds to the first awak-

Three levels on the path.

LEVEL	ORIGIN	PATH	GOAL
Symbolism	Circle	Cross	Circle
Fairy Tale	Paradise Lost	World	Paradise Regained
Psychology	Subconscious	Conscious	Super-consciousness
Jungian Psychology	Unconscious	Ego	Self
Personality Development	Simple	Developed	Unified
Consciousness	Pre-Personal	Personal	Transpersonal
State of the Ego	Lacking in Ego	Ego-bound	Free of Ego
Knowledge	Ignorant	Knowing	Wise
Understanding of Reality	Undifferentiated	Polarized	Paradox
Buddhism	Unity	Multiplicity	Wholeness
Legend of the Grail	Apple-Tree Paradise	Quest	Apple-Blossom Island,

ening of consciousness. This is always a recognition of our "sinful" nature in as far as it becomes clear to every child, and this experience is often accompanied by dismay, for the child now recognizes discomfort. Although the child may have a "better" side, it also has an aspect that is rejected or even ostracized as dirty and bad. These first tensions of opposites between good and bad, permitted and prohibited, show that the time in paradise is ending. The child will ultimately be left with the 7th card, The Chariot. Now the lengthy search for the lost unity begins.

The knowledge about the three phases of the path in life is found in a great variety of cultures, widely differing philosophies, and differing schools of thought. Since the middle section of the path always represents the development of the ego, we should be careful not to prematurely and confusingly denounce the ego. In fact, it is not a matter of avoiding its development, as some "pseudo-gurus" would like us to believe, but precisely the opposite of this. At first, it is extremely important to develop a strong ego so that the path through the outer (conscious) world can be taken. During this phase we live in separation (the inherited sin), in the forlornness of the world, in remoteness from God, or however this section may be described. Yet, we should not avoid this path, turn around, and once again become unconscious, but master it in a sincere manner. Later the task will be to overcome the ego and once again become humble and modest. This sequence of developmental steps is naturally considerably more difficult than the fearful avoidance of any development of the ego and adherence to a childlike level of consciousness.

The meaning of these phases can most easily be illustrated with the image of an iceberg, for we all know that only one-seventh can be seen while the other six-sevenths are beneath the water. If we imagine that the iceberg is completely under the water at the beginning, then this image would represent the state of complete unconsciousness at the start of life. When the tip of the ice slowly pushes itself upward, this corresponds to the wonderful awakening of the ego consciousness. This is the time when a child recognizes itself in the mirror for the first time, says "I" to itself for the first time, draws the line for the first time, and experiences itself as something different, separate from the rest of the people.

The moment when consciousness awakens, when a portion of the whole becomes conscious of itself, is something magnificent. In the briefest form, we experience it with every morning that we awaken anew. It can be easily understood why humanity has seen this perceptive power as a part of the divine Logos. In our analogy, this portion that has become aware of itself corresponds with the tip of the iceberg. If this tip were to be given an assignment, it would certainly be to recognize its own possibilities and the surrounding world, providing for orientation. But it would be absurd and presumptuous for the tip of the iceberg to claim that the goal of the journey depended upon it alone, since there is no denying that the lower six-sevenths and the currents surrounding the iceberg, are responsible for this. But it would also be completely grotesque for the tip to simply deny the lower six-sevenths and claim that there is nothing beneath the water.

The latter image corresponds somewhat with the situation of the Western mind at the beginning of the 20th century. At that time, Sigmund Freud met with incomprehension and vehement resistance in his efforts to make the subconscious "acceptable in good society." People laughed at him because they were certain that such nonsense did not exist. Since that time, this attitude has changed considerably. Today, many people accept the much more comprehensive model of C. G. Jung, in which the subconscious is no longer reduced to a deposit site for things suppressed and indecent; instead, people recognize all the forces that lead and guide the human being to exist in the unconscious mind. Applied to the image of the iceberg, it becomes clear that it is initially important to form a strong ego consciousness (the tip of the iceberg), which then must learn to not take itself so seriously, but must understand itself as the conscious but small portion of the whole. In Jungian psychology, the whole—the seven-sevenths of the iceberg—corresponds with the self, the conscious portion of which is the ego. The leading force that determines the direction is the self, while the ego is responsible for orientation, perception, and understanding. Seen in this way, Freud and Jung complement each other superbly. While Freud, with his famous saying of "where the id was, the ego shall be" emphasizes the path from the inner circle (the unconscious) to the square (the ego). The process of individuation described by C. G. Jung can be equated with "where the ego was, the self shall be" and the path from the square to the outer circle.

Within this context, it becomes easier to understand the Judaeo-Christian tradition in which Lucifer—meaning the Bringer of Light—was initially God's favorite angel. According to Gnostic sources, he was even His first son. The light that he brought to human beings was the light of knowledge. Yet, it must have been a great joy for God to experience how the light went on in His creatures and they became aware of themselves. However, according to the tradition,

Figure 12. The childhood of the hero—the symbiotic state.

Figure 13. Departure and becoming an adult—maturation and personality development.

Figure 14. The initiation process—the transpersonal opening.

Figure 15. The goal: rebirth—redemption—wholeness—
the consciousness of the unity of all things.

Lucifer soon wanted to become greater than everything and everyone else, and that led to his fall from Heaven. Since then, he has been frozen in the sea of ice of the underworld and keeps watch there as the sinister ruler of the souls that fall to him (see page 157). Although our consciousness is a divine force of perception, when it oversteps its boundaries and becomes arrogant or megalomaniac, it then changes its original beneficial force into a cold-blooded, diabolical, and power-obsessed principle.

The three previously described sections of development on the path of life are shown in the tarot through each of six cards that follow each other consecutively: I to VI (figure 12 on page 67) show us the childhood of the hero or heroine, the unconscious symbiotic phase; VII to XII (figure 13 on page 67) show the departure, the time in which he or she becomes an adult and develops an ego, and discovers individuality; XIII to XVIII (figure 14 on page 67) are the actual path of initiation, the transpersonal opening that leads to wholeness, to superconsciousness, to the unity of all things; and on to the goal of the journey, which is depicted by cards XIX to XXI (figure 15 on page 67).

If we consider the hero's journey as an allegory for the life path of a human being, it can be divided into an "obligatory section" and a "voluntary section." The 13th card, Death, is the boundary. We all come to this stage. But whether we experience death as the end or as a central theme, an essential transitional stage at the middle of our life, behind which the actual event, the initiation, the transpersonal phase, and the development of the self is waiting for us, depends upon us and what we make of our lives. However, this structure of the cards also says that we must first go through the obligatory section before we are mature enough to take part in the voluntary exercises.

Even if it appears to be very tempting to immediately become concerned with the higher things and simply overlook everything that appears to be "just" material, the message of the tarot is distinct and clear: before we turn to the transcendental areas we must learn to master reality in our everyday life. Before we overcome the ego to get to the self, we must first of all have developed an ego that is strong enough to encounter its shadow on this path without being devoured by it.

Keywords for THE CHARIOT

ARCHETYPE: The departure

TASK: Mastering contradictions, risking something new

GOAL: Experiencing the world, penetrating the unknown, accomplishing great things, succeeding in a great leap forward

RISK: Arrogance, hot-headedness, lack of self-control

FEELING IN LIFE: Optimism, desire for action, alertness, gaining consciousness, becoming an adult

he card Justice is traditionally the 8th card (see page 9) within the major arcana. However, Waite placed it in the 11th position in his deck. But since this card represents the first experiences had by a person who leaves the parental home and goes out into the world, it is in the proper place for the journey of the hero in its original 8th position. If we understand the cards as milestones on our archetypal path through life, we are at the point where we are considered to be fully responsible for ourselves, which is an essential statement of the card Justice. While at home, the customs of the clan were valid, from here on we have to learn the laws of the world. In childhood we were taken care of by the family, now we have to realize that things will go well or poorly depending on how we take care of ourselves. These are the themes of the Justice card, including the lesson that we reap what we sow; we always get what we deserve.

Justice
Maturation

Justice is shown as the form of the goddess Dike, who with her wall crown is portrayed as the protectress of the city and the order of civilization. In her right hand she holds the sword that is raised to pass and execute judgment. The right portion of the throne can be seen, as can her right foot, and law and justice are related to the right side, which is considered the rational, conscious side. All these symbols express that this is a well-considered decision, a reasonable judgment made through critical examination and on the broad basis of objective data. As the scale in her left hand shows, intuition and a sense of justice are not disregarded. However, the emphasis is upon the right, rational side. So the card Justice emphasizes the intelligent, consciously made judgment and thereby forms the complementary opposite pole to the card The Lovers, which stands for spontaneous decisions of the heart. Between these two cards stands The Chariot, which shows the entrance into the conscious phase, the step through which a well-considered, responsible judgment becomes possible in the first place. If the cards are placed next to each other, this transition can also be seen in the black sphinx—as the symbol of the unconscious—that is on the side of The Lovers, while the white (conscious) sphinx creates the connection to Justice.

Justice from the Tarot of Marseilles.

Figure 16. The Lovers: spontaneous decisions of the heart; The Chariot: becoming conscious; Justice: conscious, deliberate judgment.

In this comparison, there is no value system or interpretation that prefers one card to the other. There are situations in life that can be better decided from the heart and others that should be well-considered with the help of the critical mind. In this case, the maturing consciousness is expanded because the awakening mind is developing the ability to be decisive. Keen powers of discernment are often symbolized by a sword. Myths describe this as the moment when the still-young hero obtains his mighty sword. Siegfried, who forges Balmung—his father's broken sword—together again; Arthur, who is the only person capable of pulling Excalibur out of the rock; or Parzival, who receives his sword in his first (still unconscious) visit to the Castle of the Holy Grail.

At his departure, the hero only had a staff with him, which corresponds to the lance or the club as a symbol of courage and willpower. These are weapons like those used by two famous youths to accomplish their first bold deeds—David killed Goliath with his slingshot and Parzival conquered Ither the Red Knight with a spear. But now it is time to curb the high spirits, train the will, and go beyond the impetuous, hot-blooded thirst for action to forge a bold intellectual faculty, without which the coming tasks cannot be solved. In order for the hothead to become a knight, he must learn to carefully and deliberately weigh the consequences of his actions. Like the sword, this mental power is only found in the raw state and must be designed, formed, and sharpened before the hero can cultivate his handling of it up to the point of mastery and be dubbed a knight. Whether he then—like a Robin Hood—becomes the protector of the underprivileged and poor, or—like the Knights of the Holy Grail—becomes a spiritual seeker, or he turns into a cruel and merciless robber baron has yet to be seen.

Parzival conquers Ither with a spear [detail] (Edmund von Wörndle, Perceval Hall Vinzentium, Brixen).

Just like every sword, astuteness is also double-edged. Although reason, the power of perception, and intelligence are extremely valuable, enriching, and indispensable on the further path, the mind can also produce craftiness, meanness, and slyness, or let a person become a lying, cold-blooded, calculating, unscrupulous traitor. The powers of judgment, which this card embodies, can just as easily be misused to create prejudices and, even more, to condemn others.

Elias Canetti describes this vice as a disease of judgment so widespread among people that almost everyone is affected by it, in his opinion:

> It is the power of the *judge* that people allow themselves to act in this manner. The judge only apparently stands *between* the two camps, on the border that separates good from evil. He considers himself part of the good, in any case; the legitimization of his office is largely based on the idea that he unshakably belongs in the realm of the good, as if he were born there. He judges incessantly, so to speak. His judgment is binding. There are very specific things that he judges about; his widespread knowledge about evil and good come from long years of experience. But even those who are not judges, who no one has appointed as such, who no one in his right mind would appoint as such, ceaselessly pass judgment in all areas. Expertise is not a prerequisite

here: Those who refrain from making judgments because they are ashamed to can be counted on your fingers.[1]

One further meaning of the card Justice ensues from the generally known fact that only those can be held responsible or taken to court who are of legal age. A child is legally incapable of guilt. No one can take a child to court. On the other hand, young people—but, above all, adults—must personally be responsible for their actions to the full extent; and this is precisely what this card says. It depicts a particularly valuable aspect of the mature ego: the willingness to assume responsibility for oneself and for others. When people attempt to avoid this developmental step and persistently evade the related difficulties, they will remain immature and—regardless of age—a child. They can be easily recognized since they are never responsible for anything, are extremely bad losers, and above all, are never to blame. Instead, they develop a perfect, but ridiculous policy of blaming others so that onlookers are amazed time and again at how they manage in even the most unbelievable situations to shift the blame away from themselves and onto others. Since this is an immature, childlike consciousness, it is no wonder that its opposite can sometimes also be experienced with these people: the whiny moaning and complaining about not being worth anything and then being to blame for everything.

On the other hand, mature egos understand how to assume responsibility; where to be responsible and also how to clearly and distinctly draw the line when someone is trying to wrongly foist something on us. We can admit our own failures and still stand up for ourselves. Immature or weak egos always look enviously at others, create one-sided advantages for themselves in an obvious and shameless manner, and hardly grow beyond the childish demand of "I want it!" But mature egos can develop magnanimity, we can show ourselves to be generous, we allow good things to happen to others from the depths of the soul, we act fairly in difficult situations, we are consistent, we draw clear lines. Being able to enter into binding agreements, but also being able to just as clearly and decisively say "no" are additional valuable fruits that the mature development of the ego produces. This is precisely the task for this section of the hero's and heroine's journey. However, this demands clear powers of perception. Where, if not here, should this developmental step take place? The first half of the journey, the active path, the path of

---

[1] Elias Canetti, *Crowds and Power* (New York: Noonday Press, 1984), p. 332.

L'EMPEREUR
THE EMPEROR

LA JUSTICE
JUSTICE

Figure 17. The Emperor (IV) and his "doubling" Justice (VIII) represent the archetypal right, which dominates in patriarchal structures, from the Tarot of Marseilles.

L'IMPÉRATRICE
THE EMPRESS

L'AMOUREUX
THE LOVER

Figure 18. The Empress (III) and her "doubling" The Lover (VI) represent the archetypal left, which dominates in matriarchal structures, from the Tarot of Marseilles.

becoming conscious, is already halfway behind us. This is why the old numerical sequence of the cards (Justice = VIII) should be clearly preferred over the renumbering by Waite (Justice = XI).

In older sets of cards, such as in the Tarot of Marseilles, for example, there is an additional correlation between The Emperor—who rules with the right (rational) side, creates order, and sets limitations—and Justice—which administers justice and guards the boundaries of order. The Emperor has the number IV, the doubling of which results in VIII, the number of the card Justice (see figure 17 on page 75). The equivalent of this can be found between card III, The Empress—who rules with the left side and leads to card VI The Lovers by doubling the III, representing, in turn, the decision of the heart, which we all know beats on the left side (figure 18 on page 75). There is an interesting analogy here.

In matriarchal epochs and structures, as well as in our modern phase of childhood with its imprinting by the mother, more value was placed on morals and the judgment of the heart, the shadow aspect of which is found in misanthropic group coercion and customs, in blood vengeance and emotionally charged (lynch) judgments. Patriarchal epochs and structures, like adolescence, are dominated by substantiatable law and reasonable, well-considered judgment, the shadow aspect of which lies in hairsplitting legalism, self-righteousness, heartless severity, and a brutal dogmatism. The archetypal left can be distinguished by the sense of community and group possessions of matriarchal structures. On the other hand, the archetypal right has patriarchally characterized structures that promote the development of the ego, set lasting boundaries, and develop the personal concept of ownership.

Keywords for JUSTICE

ARCHETYPE:	Intelligence
TASK:	Understanding the laws of this world, passing an intelligent, balanced judgment, personal courage
GOAL:	Personal responsibility, objectivity, fairness and balance, intelligent perceptions
RISK:	Self-righteousness, know-it-all attitude, being prejudiced, presumption of judgment, slyness
FEELING IN LIFE:	Harvesting what one has sown, treating others and being treated fairly, making intelligent decisions

t the end of the single-digit numbers, the sun's journey ends above the daytime sky. With the motif of The Hermit, who stands on a snow-covered height, the card illustrates that the harvest of the day's journey is the highest knowledge that can be given to us on the path of becoming conscious. Myths and fairy tales portray this stage as a phase of retreat and contemplation, or tell of the encounter with the wise old man who always lives in seclusion somewhere. He gives the hero the magical tools. The hero learns from him the magic formula that protects him on his journey or—like the "Open, Sesame" —that he will need at the end in order to accomplish the great work. Above all, he learns his true name here.

The Hermit
One's True Name

This knowledge of the true name means that the hero—and therefore everyone who takes the path of becoming conscious—recognizes at this point who he truly is. And this is detached from everything that his parents, educators, relatives, or friends have told him he was up to that point. On the path of becoming conscious, this perception of true identity is the fruit that can only be found in silence and retreat. Only there can we experience who we really are. The wise old man is naturally—just as the other archetypal figures or stages—not an exterior manifestation. Even when we have the impression that this knowledge has been given to us through another person, it is still an archetypal power that has its effect within us and at best uses another person to manifest itself. It would be futile to try to meet a physical wise old man in order to have the experience that The Hermit has waiting for us, as interesting as such an encounter might be. It is much more important to hear the inner call, which in this case is always a call to silence and seclusion, and to follow it there. Only there does the old sage reveal his knowledge. Only there can we learn who we really are.

However, a growing problem in our age lies in the worldwide banishment of silence, which has now advanced to the point that it becomes increasingly difficult to find a truly quiet place where we can still hear the voice of The Hermit. As a result, fewer people learn their true name and many remain ignorant of who they really are. Instead, they become even more desperate in their attempt to imitate and portray something that they are not, something considered to be chic, en vogue, or "in." As a result, although every human being is born as an original, increasingly more people die as pure copies. C. G. Jung assesses that our innate talent of imitating others "is of the greatest utility for collective purposes [but] most pernicious for individuation."[1]

In the story of Parzival, it is his cousin Sigune who helps him become conscious. Up to now, he had answered the question of his identity as the beautiful son, the dear son, or the beautiful man, just as his mother had called him. But now he becomes aware of his true name and, in addition, of many other things he had remained completely unconscious about on his previous path. At the same time he also recognizes his guilt—the guilt of having been completely unconscious at the Castle of the Holy Grail and, because of his naive ignorance, neglecting to ask the question that redeems everything and everyone. This is why his cousin also names him "Parzival, the miserable." Since time immemorial, becoming conscious has always been accompanied by the consciousness of guilt. We cannot live without becoming guilty. No one else can occupy the place that we take at the same time. We could not feed ourselves without killing (even if this means "just" killing plants) or robbing other creatures of what belongs to them, such as milk and honey. "Looked at from the point of view of the unconscious, becoming conscious clearly appears as guilt, a genuinely tragic offence, since it is only in this way that man can become what he has to be."[2] But if the guilt of our ancestors was in eating from the Tree of Knowledge, our guilt has always been the lack of knowledge, and above all, the lack of self-knowledge. After humanity, just like the hero, has lost the paradise of innocent unconsciousness once and for all, it must solely be concerned with overcoming the twilight state of half-consciousness here—in the middle of the path. In addition, it must attain wide-awake clarity as a precondition for the breakthrough to superconsciousness, which is reserved for the last third of the path.

A further personification of this archetype in the Grail legend is Parzival's uncle Trevrezent, who lives as a recluse in a hermitage. On his longest quest, the search for the Grail, Parzival returns to this place time and again until he has found his true path. Parzival not only learns decisive things about himself from this hermit, but also the "magic for-

---

[1] C. G. Jung, "The Relation between the Ego and The Unconscious," in *Two Essays on Analytical Psychology,* CW 7, ¶ 242.
[2] Emma Jung and Marie-Louise von Franz, *The Grail Legend* (New York: Putnam, 1970), p. 205.

mula." The holy man whispers a prayer into his ear, which Parzival is only permitted to speak out loud in the moment of greatest danger.

Parzival with the Hermit, Trevrezent (detail from Parzival Cycle by Edvard Ille, Witlelsbacher Ausgleichsfond, Munich. Photo: AKG Berlin, used by permission).

Once the hero has learned his true name (and we have learned our own), he is not permitted to ever forget it and shall never deny it. In other words, once we have discovered who we truly are, the related challenge is to be true to ourselves from this day on and never again betray ourselves; otherwise, we must—like Parzival—return to this place in order to once again find ourselves. The tarot card expresses this in the shielding provided by the cowl, with which The Hermit protects himself from outside influences. Waite has interpreted his lantern as symbolizing the message: "Where I am, you also may be."[3] He therefore makes it clear that this encounter and this experience are not an exotic experience reserved for just a chosen few, but a step of consciousness that is open to every human being who goes into the silence.

The magic formula or the magical tool that the old man gives the hero to take on his journey is a present that occurs not only in fairy tales. We always are given gifts unexpectedly. The gift can be a melody, a picture, a sentence, a stone, a feather, or simply just one word, a syllable, or a symbol. It can always be recognized in that it surprisingly comes to us in quite a natural way, deeply touches us at the first moment, and there is some magical power emanating from this "gift." For rational minds, such things may sound quite curious, but they can

---

[3] A. E. Waite, *Pictorial Key to the Tarot* (York Beach, ME: Samuel Weiser, 1973), p. 104.

Hermes Trismegistus, the legendary teacher of wisdom and author of the Hermetic laws (floor mosiac, Cathedral of Sienna).

be experienced. When we are given such a gift, we should carefully guard it until we can try it out in a truly difficult situation, perhaps in a moment of fear. If we then remember the sentence, the picture, or the melody, or touch this stone or the feather, then we will feel how a great power immediately comes to help us. However, we should take to heart what the myths and fairy tales tell us about dealing with the magic formula: We cannot buy it anywhere, we also cannot just invent it; it must come to us on its own, or be bestowed upon us, and we are only permitted to use it in times of great need, never divulge it, and naturally never forget it.

How should this be understood? The unconscious possesses a "magical power," which can truly help us, particularly in difficult situations. Many people who have recognized and experienced this subjugate their unconscious mind with banalities and make it into a submissive slave through reckless "positive thinking." They want it to satisfy even the most stupid and selfish wishes of their power-hungry ego. More than 90 percent of all prayers presumably have the same goal. Certainly it would often be wise to at least thank God from the bottom of our hearts afterward when He has fortunately protected us from the fulfillment of our most foolish wishes and our most reasonable plans. However, the unconscious has "magical power" and can help us in the most wondrous way.

Naturally, it is not the sentence, the picture, or the stone itself that possesses the

Odin, the Germanic God of Wisdom, accompanied by his ravens Hugin and Munin (Hulton Deutsch Collection, London).

magical power, no more than some kind of ingenious amulet or a purchased talisman would have this magic. It is the magic that the unconscious mind has given to these things. The more we now talk this—full of pride or mystery-mongering, or if we make allusions to others or tell them our magic formula, or the more consciously we analyze our formula—the more we "wash" the magic from it. Nothing will remain but soulless formulas, empty words, dead rituals, hollow phrases, or a dead stone. The magic will disappear. This is why heros must preserve the magic formula as a treasure within. We should be

Moses, the archetype of the wise old man, receives the divine law on Mt. Sinai. This is an analogy to The Hermit's position on the peak and the divine law of the following card. (Lorenzo Ghiberti, Paradice door of Baptisterium, Florence.)

aware that this is a gift we are permitted to gratefully accept, but it is not something we have earned that our ego should boast about.

As an outstanding archetype, the wise old man in our Western culture has taken form in many famous figures. Hermes Trismegistus (Thrice-Greatest Hermes), was a legendary figure who, according to various sources, lived and taught at the dawn of ancient Egyptian advanced civilization. He was later elevated by the Egyptians to be their God of Wisdom, Thoth. He was a contemporary of Moses, as shown by the famous floor mosaic in the cathedral of Sienna. The alchemists, the Freemasons, almost all Western secret societies, and many esoteric societies call him their founding father or trace themselves back to him in some way.

Merlin, who is a key figure as the wise old man in the cycle of King Arthur legends, is even more familiar to us. Another example is Odin, the Germanic God of Wisdom, who originated from the Nordic countries. He hung on the World Ash Tree, Yggdrasil, for nine days and experienced his initiation there. As an expression of his ability to "travel in distant lands" (which means being able to go on astral journeys) that he acquired there, he has been accompanied since then by his two ravens Hugin and Munin.

An historic representative of the wise old man is Thales of Milet, a philosopher who lived in the sixth century B.C. The Greeks also called him the first of the seven wise men of the ancient world. Two of his answers to questions have been handed down to us. They are typical for a hermit. In response to the question, "What is the most difficult of all things?" he profoundly replied, "To know yourself." His response—probably with an amused smile—to the question, "What is easiest in life?" was, "Giving others good advice."

Within our Judaeo-Christian tradition, Moses is certainly the most familiar representative of this archetype. He reminded an entire people of its true identity (the true name), led them for over forty years to a predetermined goal, and gave them the divine laws. His ascent of Mt. Sinai and acceptance of the divine law finds a parallel in the transition from the tarot card The Hermit to the card The Wheel of Fortune.

Keywords for THE HERMIT

ARCHETYPE:	The wise old man
TASK:	Retreat, withdrawing into oneself, appropriate seriousness, contemplation, inner collection
GOAL:	Self-knowledge, shielding oneself from outside influences, perceiving personal standards of values, being true to oneself
RISK:	Odd character, eccentric, otherworldliness, embitterment
FEELING IN LIFE:	Clarity, inner peace, finding oneself and standing up for oneself

WHEEL of FORTUNE.

ow that the hero has become conscious of his true identity, after he has followed the daytime arc of the sun, he now seeks—at the turning point from day to night—the oracle to find an answer to the only truly important question: "What is my task?" Only now, after he has become aware of his true identity, is he mature enough to ask this question and understand the answer.

Few tarot cards are interpreted as superficially or wrongly as the Wheel of Fortune. Even Waite complained that since the days of Eliphas Levi,[1] the occult explanations of this card have been uniquely simpleminded. In fact, the meaning of the 10th tarot card is difficult to reveal if we only orient ourselves upon its name. No matter whether it is called the Wheel of Fortune or simply Luck, the name does not capture the essence of the card. A

The Wheel of Fortune
The Calling

wheel is depicted, the wheel of time. Through its continual turning, it constantly brings forth new things, while others pass in turn.

The two figures at the side of the wheel also symbolize the same thing. Both originate in Egyptian mythology: the jackal-headed Anubis, who embodies the rising, life-renewing forces, and Seth in the form of a snake, a symbol of the destructive power. In the four corners of the card, there are the four cherubim, symbolic figures for the four evangelists, who at the same time embody the four elements. Together they symbolize the entirety of Creation and are always an expression of wholeness. They appear united in the form of the sphinx who rules the wheel. It, the four-fold animal, traditionally has the face of a human, the wings of an eagle, the tail and paws of a lion, and the body of a bull. Why the wings are missing on the card in the Waite Tarot remains a puzzle since they can be clearly seen in the older sets of cards.

The alchemical symbols for salt (⊖), sulfur (🜍), mercury (☿), and water (♒) are found on the inside of the wheel. The word "Torah" is written in the outer circle with the Hebrew letters of the divine name JHVH (יהוה) between it. Considered as a whole, this symbolism

---

[1] A famous occultist of the 19th century.

As a symbol of wholeness, the sphinx unites the four elements within itself (Phoenician Sphinx from Nemrud, British Museum, London).

makes the following statement. Becoming, existing, and passing are the powers that keep the wheel of time in motion. They manifest themselves in the rising, creative aspect (Anubis), the existing, maintaining powers (sphinx), and the descending, destructive side (Seth). Together these correspond with a divine law (Torah and JHVH), which challenges human beings to transform from the base to the higher qualities (alchemical symbolism).

This means that the Wheel of Fortune represents all the tasks that we have to accomplish in our lifetime. Whenever this card appears, it says that the theme in question now enters into our life in order to be mastered. Like a mosaic, a picture gradually grows from all these individual aspects; it lets us sense our task in life at the beginning, but with time, it becomes increasingly clear. However, this does not mean that it will ever let itself be reduced to one term or one formula. It can be described in pictorial terms, as oracles have done since time immemorial, when they answer the hero's question about his task in life with the profound response: "Seek the treasure that is hard to find!"

If we want to understand this answer in psychological terms, there is an illuminating explanation given by C. G. Jung. We have him to thank for a characterology that appears to be quite similar to older typologies at first glance. Jung also differentiates between the four basic structures in human consciousness, which he calls the functions of consciousness—thinking, feeling, sensing, and intuition. They are similar to classical models of the four, like the four elements (fire, earth, air, and water), or the four temperaments (sanguine, choleric, melancholy, and phlegmatic. However, Jung puts an emphasis on the dynamic that is unique to Jungian typology. While other characterologies sometimes have something "fixed" about them, and describe a person once and for all as a certain type or mixed type, Jung assumes that the consciousness of every human being consists of all four aspects; however, these are not all developed in the same way. To the contrary, as C. G. Jung recognized from a great variety of traditions, from myths and fairy tales, from alchemical symbolism, and, of course, naturally from his work as a physician and therapist, that the human being usually only develops three of these four functions of consciousness during the first half of life. The fourth remains in the realm of the unconscious. It corresponds to the fairy-tale motif of the soul that has been sold, or the pearl (a symbol of wholeness) that is lost at the beginning of the story. The hero's double set of parents, who reflect his origin and his abilities, are a foursome, and represent the wholeness that is innate to the hero. However, one of the

The Oracle of Delphi.

four persons will generally be experienced as the "stepmother" and treated accordingly in a neglectful manner. According to Jung, turning toward this neglected side, exploring it, and "raising it from the depths" is the theme of the second half of life. It corresponds, in a psychological sense, with the treasure that is hard to find.

How should this be understood? We apparently develop our strengths only to the detriment of our weak aspects. The more strongly one of the three developed functions of consciousness distinguishes itself, the more deeply the fourth function will be suppressed into the unconscious mind and is therefore lacking in our consciousness. This makes it a source of our failures, which frequently causes us to be dissatisfied and unhappy.

C. G. Jung called this most strongly developed aspect of consciousness the main function of a human being. The two following, likewise conscious functions—which, in contrast to the simplified model on page 90, are usually developed to varying degrees—are called the first and second auxiliary functions. The unconscious aspect, the treasure that is hard to find, is the inferior, least valued function.

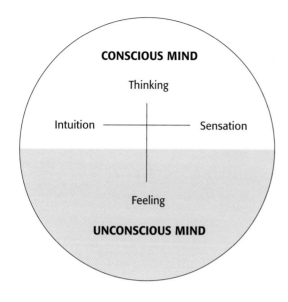

CONSCIOUS MIND

Thinking

Intuition ———|——— Sensation

Feeling

UNCONSCIOUS MIND

Figure 19. The Thinking Type.

If, for example, a person has developed a strong thinking function, then feeling is usually the function that he neglects. Depicted in a simplified manner, the model will look like figure 19.

However, this initial imbalance does not mean that a developmental error is involved and it would be better for a person, if possible, to develop all four aspects of consciousness to an equal extent from the very start. According to everything that we can perceive, it appears natural, good, and right to develop three of these functions at first, and then intensively confront the missing aspect during the second half of life, just as the hero's journey only leads to the treasure that is hard to find during the second half of the path. The tasks that result for the four different types appear to be—when seen from the psychological perspective—as follows.

People who correspond to the above model are generally considered "overly cerebral." If they were asked to spontaneously say what they feel, they would immediately reply: "I think, I feel . . ." For them, thinking is so much quicker than any feeling, they always have an answer in a flash. So these people imagine what they could appropriately feel in a given situation. However, it would be wrong to conclude that they cannot feel this response as well. They just need much more time to do it. Their feeling function is underdeveloped, sticky, raw, generalized, and not as wonderfully differentiated and immediately available as is this thinking function. This is why they feel it to be so annoying to deal with this level. As it has not been developed, or is just slightly developed and has something simple and primitive about it, there is nothing here of which they can be proud. By way of contrast to this, their thinking is brilliant. This is why they much prefer to show themselves from this civilized side, but also tend to have a rather disdainful opinion of their underdeveloped area—feeling—which they then experience as inferior. They basically think that humanity could do without it, if necessary. In the second half of life, time and again these people will experience situations that will challenge them to accept feelings and develop emotions.

In a world where there are "overly cerebral" people, there is no lack of individuals who have "gut feelings." These are the people whose feeling function is so highly developed that they are extremely quick to pass a judgment or form an opinion on the basis of a gut feeling. For them, the model of consciousness appears as in the illustration of the feeling type (figure 20).

At the least, they have neglected thinking and have a hard time providing reasons for their emotional judgments or explaining something in a logical manner. They would vehemently dispute someone saying they are not not able to "think." This is particularly the case

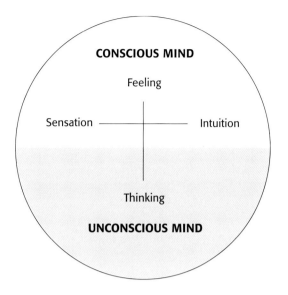

Figure 20. The Feeling Type.

because our society so one-sidedly glorifies thinking that such a statement would be like a devastating judgment. But what the feeling type experiences as thinking is pure wishful thinking, or an outstanding sureness of instinct, but not what corresponds with logical, analytical, and consistent thought.

This means that the treasure that is hard to find for "overly cerebral" individuals would be feeling, whereby the "gut-feeling" types must learn sober thinking oriented toward objective perceptions.

The sensation types perceive the world through the senses—color, taste, smell, and outer form. They can abandon themselves to this sensory pleasure, or solely fixate on the outer form, and they lose any feeling of what possibilities lie in an object or a plan. They lack the intuitive access. In extreme cases, they only see what is, and not what is possible. Developing this nose, feeling what possibilities this world has to offer in its variety, creating a sense for trends and estimating the opportunities that an experiment or undertaking may have—in short, opening their inner eye, is their lost treasure (see figure 21 on page 92).

Their polarities experience the world in exactly the opposite manner. Intuition types are so fascinated by the possibilities that lie within an idea, an object, or a project that they completely neglect the form

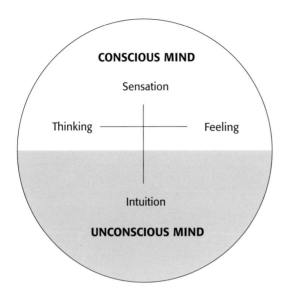

Figure 21. The Sensation Type.

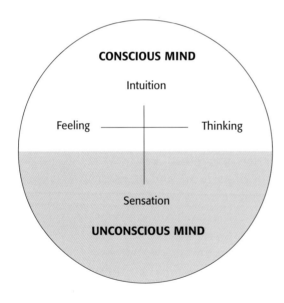

Figure 22. The Intuition Type.

and the actual facts as a result. Wrapped up in fantasies, they rarely get around to making something of it. Making friends with sober reality, not being content to just have a vision of things, but developing the patience to let the vision become concrete and to translate it into action is their lost treasure (figure 22).

In the tarot cards, the cherubim, the four symbolic figures in the corners of the cards, represent the four elements—fire, earth, air, and water. In turn, these correspond to the four functions that have been described earlier in the form of the four temperaments. All four hold books in their hands as symbols of the tasks and lessons they will impart. Whenever a person asks the question, "What are my tasks in this life?," one of the four figures will answer, "Learn about me, develop my essential nature so that you become whole."

At the end of the major arcana is The World as the 21st card. It corresponds to the outer circle of the mandala (see page 62), the regained paradise in the fairy tales and legends. On the spiritual level, it represents the attained wholeness as the goal of all our lives. The four cherubim can be seen here again, but in contrast to the 10th card, they no longer hold books in their hands. This means that the lessons of the Wheel of Fortune have been learned on the path between the two, wholeness has been achieved, the person has become healed, and the missing fourth force has been integrated (see figure 23).

Figure 23. In the Wheel of Fortune, the cherubim hold books in their hands, and they impart lessons; in The World, the cherubim have no books in their hands, for the lessons have been learned.

With the Wheel of Fortune, we have reached the two-digit cards. On the journey of the sun, it corresponds with the setting sun on the Western horizon, an image of turning the light to the dark and previously neglected polarity. This moment also illustrates the term of necessity in the sense of a compulsive law, as well as with regard to the turning point that the sun must inevitably perform here. The experiences that we have in relation to this card are also necessary and inevitable.

Seen symbolically, "masculine" corresponds to what separates, and "feminine" to what binds. To the same extent, the traveled masculine stretch of the path separates us from the origin, whereas the feminine stretch of the path that lies before us unites us with it. Masculine thinking is separating, differentiating thought that always sets new limits and crystallizes increasingly finer differences; on the other hand, the feminine, analogous thinking is holistic, recognizes and emphasizes common grounds, and thereby repeals the boundaries that were drawn before. Masculine thought accuses feminine thought of being ambiguous, while feminine thought laughs at the entire masculine struggle for clarity, knowing well that reality is too complex to ever be subjected to a clear formula.[2] The covered path of single-digit

---

[2] This naturally does not refer to the thinking of man and woman. Masculine and feminine are to be understood as symbolic terms like yin and yang (see table on page 34 for further details).

Figure 24. The Magician embodies the strength and skill to master the tasks; while the Wheel of Fortune symbolizes the task in life.

cards leads away from the unity of the origin to the multiplicity in which the awakened, developing ego ultimately becomes increasingly one-sided in the constant struggle for clarity. However, the path through the two-digit numbers that now lies before us—even if it is often initially disdained for its ambiguity—will ultimately lead us through paradoxical perceptions to the unity of all things. This is because "oddly enough the paradox is one of our most valued spiritual possessions, while uniformity of meaning is a sign of weakness," says C. G. Jung, and (somewhat later) he continues, "only the paradox comes anywhere near to comprehending the fullness of life. Non-ambiguity and non-contradiction are one-sided and thus unsuited to express the incomprehensible."[3]

The ego does not at all like the change of direction that becomes necessary here. It really hates giving up its claim to being the only one capable of clearly explaining everything. Perhaps this is one reason why oracles are sometimes prematurely interpreted incorrectly. The two ways of reacting to the required change of course can be seen in the patriarchal and matriarchal manner of reading the following card (Strength). The refusal to carry out the change of course demanded

---

[3] C. G. Jung, *Psychology and Alchemy*, CW, vol.12, ¶ 15.

here, which is frequently encountered, always leads to the apparently hopeless dilemma of The Hanged Man.

The two-digit cards of the major arcana are always connected in meaning with the cards to whose cross sum they correspond (figure 24). In this case, it is the 10th card (Wheel of Fortune) that leads to the 1st card (The Magician). While the Wheel of Fortune embodies the lifework, The Magician symbolizes the skill and strength to accomplish the tasks set. Consequently, the task in life for every human being is created in such a way that it can be accomplished and mastered.

Keywords for WHEEL OF FORTUNE

ARCHETYPE: The calling, the prediction

TASK: Insight into what is necessary, facing one's tasks

GOAL: Transforming what is base into something higher, mastering the lifework, becoming whole

RISK: Fatalism, misunderstanding one's tasks

FEELING IN LIFE: Experiences and events that allow us to become whole, even if we initially dislike them.

trength is one of the two cards whose position A. E. Waite exchanged—contrary to the traditional order (see page 9). In its original 11th position, it opens the second decade of the major arcana as the feminine counterpart to The Magician, with which the first decade begins. The similarities between both cards are apparent and highlighted in the Waite Tarot by the same coloration. In both cases, the theme is strength. The Magician personifies creative power, influential strength, and mastery, while Strength expresses vitality, passion, and the joy of life (see figures 25 and 26 on page 98). There is a lemniscate (∞), the infinity sign, above the head of the figure on both of the cards. In the Tarot of Marseilles, this is hidden in the form of the hats.

This infinity sign symbolizes the constant connection and alternating exchange of the two

Strength

Hubris or the Helpful Animal

levels, or worlds. For The Magician, it represents the connection between above and below, between macrocosm and microcosm, while on the Strength card, it stands for the harmonious connection of the civilized person (woman) with her animal nature (lion). For all these reasons, feminine strength stands at the beginning of the feminine stretch of the path, which will lead to the secrets of the depths in the course of the two-digit cards. This is naturally much more convincing here in the 11th position than in the 8th.

The meaning of this card on the hero's journey depends upon the interpretation that we choose for it—the patriarchal or the matriarchal. The lion is the symbol of our instinctual and impulsive nature, our passionate, wild, aggressive urges and the naked self-preservation drive. Patriarchal myths tell of heroes who kill the lions, whereby the most familiar of these stories, interestingly enough, do not end well for them. Samson became the victim of a ruse and lost all his strength; the glorious Heracles also had considerable problems, mostly with his feminine side. In an initial attack of insanity, he killed his wife and children; after another act of insanity, he was sentenced to assume the role of a woman as atonement. So he served in women's clothing in the court of the Lydian Queen Omphale for three years. He had to spin and do other kinds of women's work, while she wore his lion's

Figure 25. The Magician and Strength from the Waite Tarot.

Figure 26. The Magician and Force from the Tarot of Marseilles.

skin and carried his club. Although this "therapy" helped him to integrate his suppressed side to the extent that he was freed from his insanity, his injured inner femininity was still not completely healed by it. The remaining wound ultimately cost him his life.

In this lion-killing, patriarchal variation of the story, the card corresponds with hubris, self-conceit and our impudent refusal to subject ourselves to divine law and fulfill the tasks assigned to us. But here it is necessary to conquer the dragon in the feminine way, which means accepting it.[1]

Fortunately, the tarot has preserved this message for us in the picture, which shows a woman who lovingly tames the lion. This motif has only been passed down in mythological fragments, but was apparently quite popular during matriarchal epochs. The great Sumerian goddess Inanna, who corresponds with Venus, was depicted standing on a lion that she had tamed; it was often said that her Babylonian "successor," Ishtar, was a lion. The Greek goddess Artemis was also considered a lioness of women. Only with the increasing denouncement of our instinctual and impulsive nature in the Christian religion did the lion increasingly become a symbol of the Antichrist, who is trod underfoot by the Holy Virgin. This reflects the attempt of consciousness to get a grip on, to enslave, or even kill the animal within us that is rejected from now on as sinful. "Mere suppression of the shadow," as Jung remarked in probably a somewhat ironic manner, "is

---

[1] Cf. Erich Neumann, *Amor and Psyche: The Psychic Development of the Feminine* (Princeton: Princeton University Press, 1970), p. 132.

Heracles spins wool while dressed in women's clothing. The Lydian Queen has taken away his club and lion's skin (Bartholomaeus Spranger, Kunsthistorisches Museum, Vienna; used by permission).

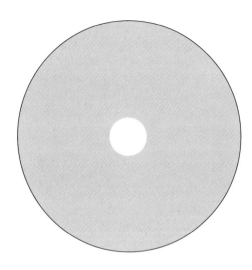

Figure 27. Consciousness, surrounded by the unconscious.

as little of a remedy as beheading would be for a headache."[2]

However, in dealing with our dark side, our inner wildness, and when encountering the inner animal, it would be just as inappropriate to play them down, or avoid and suppress them, as it would be to approach them with rigidity or violence. There is a good reason why this encounter only takes place now, at the middle section of the path. Up to this point, it has been important to develop and adequately strengthen the ego powers so that they can withstand this confrontation, for an ego consciousness that is too weak could easily be devoured by the forces of the unconscious mind. C. G. Jung repeatedly pointed out how misleading it is to speak of the subconscious, because this term awakens the impression that there would be a spacious conscious self that has no difficulty in controlling everything unconscious. Instead, Jung preferred to speak of the unconscious, the relation of which to consciousness he depicted as something like figure 27.

The consciousness that humanity has developed during the course of a few millennia, and that every human being must develop anew in the course of his or her own life, is completely surrounded by the unconscious. If it is so weak that boundaries become permeable, the unconscious can uninhibitedly inundate consciousness. The so-called primitive peoples call this occurrence the loss of the soul. In quite a vivid way, we speak in this case of mental derangement. In order to be a match for this danger, the ego must become strong and mature on the first stretch of the path. It must be solidly rooted in outer reality in order to be capable of a dialog with unconscious forces in order to hold its own in the coming encounters. Otherwise, the ego will be too easily engulfed, inundated, or washed away by the feelings, fantasies, and images of the unconscious. For this reason, in myths and fairy tales, the true hero can only be the person who has consciously encountered the danger without letting himself or herself be

---

[2] C. G. Jung, "Psychology and Religion," in *Psychology and Religion: West and East*, CW, vol. 4, ¶ 133.

devoured by the night, or the monster, in the process.

One of the great mythological figures who did not fight against inner wildness, but embodied it as a divine force, was Dionysus. He even knew how to ride the wild animal.

Dionysus was the god of intoxication, of wine, and of wild, orgiastic festivals. Mythology reports that he—a child of the city of Thebes—went off to distant lands at an early age. As a handsome young man, he returned home with a wild horde of musicians and Bacchantes from Asia Minor in order to bring his cult to Thebes. But since the dancing mob was not very welcome there, his people moved on to the gates of the city, drumming, singing, and whistling in order to set up their camp on the

Dionysus riding on a panther (Hellenistic mosiac, Delos. Photo: by permission of Leo Maria Giani, Munich).

slopes of Mt. Kithaeron. And then something strange happened. Fascinated by the irresistibility of the god, increasingly more women left their homes secretly at night and crept out of the city to celebrate with Dionysus in the woods.

Pentheus, the honorable King of Thebes, thought this wild cult was an outrage. When Dionysus appeared to him one day as a young man, the king immediately had him thrown into the dungeon. However, the god escaped from it in a miraculous manner. Once again, he appeared to the king, seductively told him of the orgiastic festivals, and described with relish the details of the permissive debauchery. In this manner, he knew how to awaken the lascivious curiosity of the king in such a way that he was easily enticed and let himself be talked into putting on women's clothing to reach the camp of the Bacchantes unrecognized from the city. Once there, he hid himself in a tree, from which he could observe the wild activities. What he saw was so overwhelming that his eyes nearly popped out of his head and he became totally dazed. However, this caused him to become so incautious that the ecstatically dancing women noticed him. In their intoxication, they thought he was a mountain lion. So they rushed at him, dragged him from the tree, tore him to pieces while he was still alive, speared his head on a Bacchus staff, and set out for the city singing and dancing with this trophy. Only when they arrived there did this mania fall away from them. The woman who carried the staff was Agave, the king's mother; she was horrified to discover that she had torn her own son to pieces.

Such stories show how dangerous it can be to enslave, suppress, or even kill the animal within us (the inner wildness). To the extent to which we suppress something or believe we have it under control, the danger of becoming a victim of this denounced aspect increases. Had Pentheus given his animalistic nature enough room in his life, he would have been familiar with it and would have been able to direct it. Instead, he was overpowered in the truest sense of the word by a suppressed, and thereby largely unconscious, lustfulness that he believed he could control.

If we approach the animal in a careful and friendly way, it will frequently become an allied, helpful force. In many fairy tales, the animal is often wild and dangerous at the beginning and must first be tamed. The hero who succeeds in doing this, and then trusts the animal's guidance, finds the treasure or whatever should be found. Marie-Louise von Franz has studied a multitude of fairy tales to see whether they make a common, unchanging statement, an irrefutable recommendation as to how a human being should behave in a certain situation. But this effort was in vain since there apparently is no such absolute truth for the collective unconscious, the original source from which the fairy tales come. The advice is totally dependent upon the situation and even then, it differs in the most comparable circumstances. Just one single rule appears to be without exception: whoever hurts the helpful animal will always meet with misfortune![3]

To survive on the further path, consciousness must then find the right attitude toward the unconscious. It must learn to trustingly let itself be guided and, above all, not follow any ambitious or greedy goals of the ego. If the ego refuses to engage in this "exercise of humility," attempting instead with shrewd tricks to rob the unconscious mind of its magical power so that it seizes this power for itself, then it is lacking what is authentic.[4] Then the human being becomes enslaved

---

[3] Marie-Louise von Franz, *Shadow and Evil in Fairy Tales* (Zurich: Spring, 1974), pp. 119–120.

[4] "Missing the authentic" is a further interpretation of the word "sin." Interestingly enough, the 11, the number of this card, is also the number of sin.

by his or her fantasies of omnipotence and fails on the journey into the underworld: he or she subsequently becomes an animal. In the typical fairy-tale motif of three brothers or three sisters, these are usually the obstacles at which the two older siblings fail, while the simpleton has a "pure heart" and can therefore accomplish the work.

The Bible tells us the same thing about the Babylonian king Nebuchadnezzar, who, disregarding the warning he received in a dream, boasted smuggly on the roof of his palace: "Look how great Bablyon is! I built it as my capital city to display my power and might, my glory and majesty." (Daniel 4:30). Even while these words were still on his lips, the king turned into an animal and had to "live with wild donkeys and eat grass like an ox" (Daniel 5:21).

What makes the path into the depths so dangerous? Why does the human being fear the descent into darkness? Above all, our consciousness feels attracted to whatever awakens the appearance of order because it believes it can see through this phenomenon, gauge it, and also be able to control it sooner or later. This is why we like to speak of the divine order, and at the same time leave everything coincidental and chaotic to the Devil. We encounter these denounced, meaning

The degenerated King Nebuchadnezzar, who turned into an animal (William Blake, Tate Gallery, London).

Figure 28. The High Priestess—the willingness to get involved; Strength—the encounter with the instinctual and impulsive nature.

unpredictable, aspects on the path through the two-digit cards. The path stands—as we saw at the beginning—under the guidance of The High Priestess, who embodies both the art of being able to let things happen, as well as the willingness to get involved.

In the original numbering, Strength, the first card of the feminine path, corresponds to The High Priestess through its cross sum (see figure 28). This correlation lets us recognize once again that "nothing more can be done" on the remainder of the path. Actually, The Magician's active section of the path has ended and we now wait to let things "happen." The Magician led us from the mother's womb out into the world. Activity was demanded on this section of the path, and it was important to skillfully master the tasks. Here, in the middle of the journey, the portents have changed. The High Priestess now takes over the guiding role, which means gradually giving back all the masculine symbols of power that were so strenuously gained on the previous stretch of the path. The stabilized, matured, but power-hungry ego must recognize its boundaries, once again becoming humble and modest. Up to now, the hero had to *have* experiences, but now the challenge is to *be open* to experiences with a full heart. From now on, nothing more will come when the ego wants it and because it wants it, but when and because the self wants it. From here on, nothing more can be forced. All further experiences elude planning. They come at their own time and cannot be determined at workshops or weekend seminars. The essential being occurs involuntarily in the truest sense, and—as long as the time is not ripe—absolutely nothing will happen no matter how long we remain in the perfect headstand, devout prayer, or motionless meditation while letting ourselves be engulfed with incense or sweet New Age sounds. The second half of the path that begins here *can* lead the hero to a view of the Highest; however, this only happens when he or she has already mastered the demands of the first half.

From this point on, there is nothing more to be learned from the cleverest of books, only getting involved with heart and soul in the experiences to which we are led will work. This is where the alchemical formula, "rend the books lest your hearts be rent asunder"[5] belongs, which C. G. Jung considered to be so decisive, "lest thinking impair feeling and this hinder the return of the soul."[6] Here at the latest, the intellect must comprehend its function in the positive sense as a "head office," as the central headquarters and control station that supervises instead of "violating," that furnishes the various aspects of our personality with coordinated expression instead of commanding, tyrannizing, or flatly suppressing the unpleasant aspects. Above all, the essential task of this control station lies in perceiving what is happening and in the insight—which is very significant—that running away is not a solution.

All of this makes this path uncertain and uncomfortable. Just as hesitantly as we took our first steps out into life on the previous stretch of the path, we stand at the same point again. Something completely unknown lies ahead of us. And not only this: much of what we are now familiar with on the path within will play mischief with what had appeared to be obvious and proven up to now. It will irritate and frighten us. Within this context, C. G. Jung compared the child's fear of the big, wide world with the fear that we experience when we come into contact with our still childlike inner side, a world that is just as wide and unfamiliar. This fear, he says, "is legitimate insofar as our rational *Weltanschauung* with its scientific and moral certitudes—so hotly believed in because so deeply questionable—is shattered by the facts of the other side."[7]

The Greeks called their underworld the realm of the shadows. And that is precisely where the journey takes us. It was C. G. Jung who introduced the term "shadow" to psychology in order to describe the sum of our unlived, and usually unloved, possibilities. In the shadow lies everything that we apparently do not have, but oddly enough seem to constantly perceive in others. Whenever we instantaneously become outraged or sulkily feel ourselves to be misunderstood, when someone suggests that we have made mistakes, or when we react to criticism with an irritation that can hardly be suppressed, we can be certain that we have come into contact with a part of our shadow.

If this were not the case, criticisms or accusations would not hit us so hard. Then we could and would calmly but resolutely make it

---

5 *Rosarium Philosophicum*, an alchemical work from 1550.
6 C. G. Jung, "Psychology of the Transference," in *The Practice of Psychotherapy*, CW, vol. 16, ¶ 488.
7 C. G. Jung, "The Relation between the Ego and the Unconscious," in *Two Essays on Analytical Psychology*, CW, vol. 7, ¶ 324.

clear that there must be some misunderstanding here. But as soon as the shadow, our unloved aspect, is touched upon, the ego immediately sounds the alarm. It is annoyed and dogged as it denies all the accusations, especially since the reproach can actually point to a characteristic that lies so far in the shadow of consciousness that the ego really knows nothing of it. But just the fact of experiencing something foreign to the ego does not prove that it does not belong to us; it only proves that we know nothing of it. In the process, above all, the degree of indignation is an interesting yardstick for determining whether a reproach or an accusation conceals a shadow theme.

Since the shadow contains all the possibilities that we have but do not live out because of cultural, moral, or personal reasons, it includes the entire "inner human being" with all its possibilities. This is why the shadow realm is not limited to outlawed themes. Instead, here are also the possibilities that we find to be completely positive and worth striving for, but at the same time seem to be so inconceivable to us that our ego just cannot get an idea of them. They appear too big, too risky, or too extraordinary to us so that we do not think ourselves capable of them. We could call them the light part of the shadow.

Confrontation with the shadow requires courage and strength since we ultimately encounter a strong side of ourselves that is unknown to us. This is a very central portion of the maturation process in which we can learn important things about ourselves. In fact, every ego possesses the quite special skill of putting itself in a thoroughly favorable light over and over, without any difficulty, at least, in relation to the comparative group. It is astounding to see how even the most rotten scoundrels and worst criminals effortlessly succeed in doing this. Whether it be an unscrupulous drug deal, a cold-blooded tyrant, a fraudulent bankrupt, or a merciless torturer—none of these egos have any problem at all in designing a surprisingly positive picture of their own person, and shifting the blame for all the evil onto other people, acts of God, or compelling circumstances.

However, as long as we just try to put ourselves into the right light, we follow—free of any type of self-criticism—a naive urge of the ego. But we cannot find our wholeness without having recognized and accepted that the shadow also belongs to it. Some of us may find this relatively easy to do when these are gigantic shadow figures. In the process, the ego may even show pride in confessing to having an abysmally evil side and, for example, having the ability to be a warmonger feared by everyone, a terrible mass murderer, or a horrible dictator. These people are always given more space in later history books than the upright and the good.

Shadow integration becomes much more unpleasant for most people, especially when we must admit the most banal shabbiness to ourselves; embarrassments that cause us to be ashamed to the bone, and we hope that no one will ever catch us in them. It is difficult to see that it is not the neighbor, but we, ourselves, who are the cowards, the thieves, the vicious liars, the lousy little philistines, the nasty schemers, or simply just phony, spineless, conformist worms; that we have all the desires, cravings, addictions, and weaknesses of which we like to accuse others in order to hypocritically condemn them; that we are not at all as noble, helpful, and good as we like to think we are. All of this is very, very difficult for us. But without the shadow there would be no clear profile. "The living form needs deep shadow if it is to appear plastic," says C. G. Jung. "Without shadow it remains a two-dimensional phantom, a more or less well brought-up child."[8] And in another section, he points out that, "It is certainly no ideal for people always to remain childish, to live in a perpetual state of delusion about themselves, foisting everything they dislike on to their neighbours and plaguing them with their prejudices and projections."[9]

However, at the center of the confrontation with the unconscious shadow world stands the encounter with the inner opposite sexuality. As Jung has shown, the unconscious of the man behaves in a feminine manner (he called it the *anima*) and the unconscious of the woman behaves in a masculine manner (he called it the *animus*). Becoming aware of this unconscious opposite sexuality, encountering it, and accepting it is an essential portion of the journey within. As long as we are fascinated by this opposite sexuality "out there" in the other sex, we are naturally enthusiastic about it. But as soon as it becomes important to inwardly accept it as our own, the crisis begins. A man who encounters his feminine side that has been hidden from him up to now will first experience it just as weakness, softness, cowardice, and helplessness. So he "naturally" decides to remain hard. At this point in time, he does not yet realize that this inner femininity ultimately can and will lead him to a view of the Highest. And the weaker his ego is, the more it will fear failure, and the tougher it believes it must act toward the outside world. Instead of inner solidity, it develops only external hardness, behind which inner sponginess and extreme over-sensitivity is concealed. The type of man who is often and quickly insulted is capable of extreme brutality, if only to

---

[8] C. G. Jung, *Two Essays on Analytical Psychology*, CW, vol. 7, ¶ 400.
[9] C. G. Jung, "Psychology of the Transference," in *The Practice of Psychotherapy*, CW, vol. 16, ¶ 420.

Achilles kills Penthesilea (vase, Antiquity Collection, Munich).

compensate for his inner softness. Instead of accepting his femininity and maturing as a result, he tends to fight against it everywhere.

A famous representative of this type of character is the Greek hero Achilles. He clung to his mother, the nymph Thetis, all his life. She had wanted to make him immortal by immersing him as a newborn in the River Styx (the name means "hate"). As she did this, the heel by which she was holding him remained unprotected. Mercilessly tough toward the outside world, but inwardly extremely sensitive, frequently sulking, and often resentful, Achilles was considered one of the most capable, but also one of the cruelest, warriors in the Battle of Troy. Yet, instead of connecting with his anima, which he encountered in the figure of the Amazon Queen Pen-thesilea, he killed her. Only then did he fall so desperately in love with her corpse that he violated it. His story has an appropriately bad ending: he let the secret of his vulnerable Achilles' heel be coaxed out of him by the beautiful Polyxena. Soon thereafter, he became the victim of a conspiracy. Whenever the ego dreams of a victory over the anima or animus, danger threatens since "every encroachment of the ego is followed by an encroachment from the unconscious."[10]

The situation is similar for a woman who is unaware of her inner masculinity and instead fights it in the outside world. Because she doesn't trust in her own masculinity, she either experiences everything masculine in the outside world as so threatening that it must be destroyed, or she falls completely into the role of being helpless and a victim. Then she battles—no less efficiently—by constantly causing her masculine world in particular to have a bad conscience. Since the patriarchal order denies a woman open, aggressive forms of expression, this latter type of

---

[10] C. G. Jung, "The Relation between the Ego and the Unconscious," in *Two Essays on Analytical Psychology*, CW, vol. 7, ¶ 382.

woman, who fights indirectly, plays the "classical" role of woman in a patriarchal society. On the other hand, the first type is described in Jungian psychology as the castrating woman. She either "castrates" the man at her side in the area of the upper masculinity (head) or the lower masculinity (sex) by constantly cutting him short, patronizing him, treating him like a stupid boy, or sexually withdrawing from him. All of this is not conscious behavior that could be seen as evil or ill-willed, but rather an immature, unconscious way of living out an inner problem. Because the behavior is naive, it is not "bad," but there comes a time when the woman needs to become mature and confront her own unconscious.

Heracles and Hippolyta (vase, Museo Civico, Barletta, Italy).

These feminine problems have a certain correlation in the Heracles myth, which tells us of the deadly battle with another Amazon queen, Hippolyta, a daughter of the god Ares. As the ninth of his twelve tasks, Heracles must obtain Hippolyta's girdle. So he sails to the land of the Amazons. In the form of an ultimatum, he demands that the girdle, the sign of tribal dominion, be handed over to him. Without any hesitation, Hippolyta is actually willing to voluntarily give him this symbol of her power; yet, Hera, the jealous enemy of Heracles, permits him no such easy victory. In the form of an Amazon, she incites all the other Amazon warriors to attack the hero. Incensed at this treachery, the hero kills the queen, who has broken her word in his eyes.

If we read the message of this legend from the feminine perspective, it tells us of a very masculine woman who is determined to connect herself with the animus in a positive manner. In this process, the queen is the bearer of consciousness, while her people symbolize the various aspects of her essential nature. But this woman is not yet a united personality; she fails to recognize fundamental forces within herself. Consciously, she was certainly quite willing to do without the outer symbols of her power and surrender to her opposite pole. But she underestimated the strength and strong individuality of the various parts of her essential nature that had not yet been integrated. These portions—incited by an archetypal force—caused the intentions of consciousness to fail. This also applies to Odysseus, whose return home fails time and again because of his companions—his non-integrated aspects—until he ultimately can return to his homeland alone, meaning unified (see page 200). He was permitted three tries. On the other hand, fate only granted one attempt to Hippolyta.

Interestingly enough, the myths tell us time and again that the great work can only be accomplished by someone who has a living relationship with the opposite sex. We can see how important this constant connection is for Odysseus, who would have been lost without Circe, as well as Perseus and Athene, Theseus and Ariadne, Dante and Beatrice, Inanna and Ninshubur, and many others. This confrontation between man and woman is apparently an indispensable catalyst for self-knowledge and development of the self for every human being. Perhaps it even means that instead of having the task of lifting us into seventh heaven, our love relationships are intended to be the framework for important developmental steps.[11] Incidentally, the same applies not only to the relationship between man and woman but also between adult and child. In any case, we can conclude from the archetypal pictures that the disappointed refusal to continue to deal with the other sex ("I'm fed up once and for all with men/women!") means the same as stagnation, a dead end, and decay. It certainly does not lead to true maturity, or even to accomplishing our task in life.

At the end of the masculine path of becoming conscious stands self-knowledge (The Hermit) as the highest fruit. To know who we really are was the goal of the first half of the path (and an unrenouncable precondition for the second). There are no further heights to climb there. Instead, the absolutely essential turning point followed with the Wheel of Fortune, which opened the path into the depths, down to the treasure that is hard to find. But if the conscious mind that has become proud and self-assured refuses to participate in this turning point, this would be like a sun that refused to set, and instead kept moving further and further toward the west. It would very quickly forfeit and lose any contact with Earth.

---

11 Cf. Hajo Banzhaf and Brigitte Theler, *Secrets of Love and Partnership* (York Beach, ME: Samuel Weiser, 1998), p. 25ff.

People whose thinking has something strangely distant to it appear just as detached and without any relation to earthly reality. They sound overly clever, abstract, and lifeless. It appears that they have not succeeded in finding the turning point and have remained one-sided. They lack the Dionysian depth that makes us feel what they want to express; they lack the sensuality that can only develop on the lower path; they lack the passion that this card embodies. They have missed the turning point or believe that other rules apply to them. Instead, they must still get the "hang" of things, in the truest sense of the word, in order to grow in the depths. This is the theme of the next card.

Keywords for STRENGTH

ARCHETYPE:	Taming the animal
TASK:	Enjoyable acceptance of life, courage and commitment
GOAL:	Joy of living, holy passion, encounter with one's own instinctive nature and inner wildness
RISK:	Hubris, hardening, brutality
FEELING IN LIFE:	Feeling totally alive, being passionately committed, and—when necessary—also showing one's claws

THE HANGED MAN.

he Hanged Man usually leaves a lasting impression on most people. Almost anyone who holds this card for the first time turns it around a few times before becoming clear about the right way to hold it. The Hanged Man is characteristically hung by the foot with his head hanging downward in all the classical tarot portrayals. This was the punishment for traitors in the Middle Ages. And this actually is a matter of betrayal in a certain sense: betrayal of one's own affairs, the betrayal of ourselves. The Hanged Man represents the deadend street on which we are stuck, the trap that we walk into when we are on the wrong path. Translated into the terms of the hero's journey, this means that the hero has apparently overshot the goal of the day's journey. He has refused to set out on the journey through the night and will therefore be forced by fate to turn around.

The Hanged Man
The Great Crisis

From the symbolism of this card, we can read where the actual problem lies. The Hanged Man forms a cross with his legs, while the position of the arms corresponds to a triangle. Like the square, the cross stands for the number 4. Together with these two figures, the four has signified the earthly realm since time immemorial. On the other hand, the triangle, as well as the number 3, symbolizes the divine. This means the position of The Hanged Man is a symbol of the upside-down world in which he hangs; a world in which the divine is below and the earthly realm is above. In other words: what is real, essential, and significant is buried beneath the earthly realm and this is why the human being is stuck at this point. If we were to meet someone in such an awkward situation, we would certainly give him the good advice of simply turning around. Then he would be standing the right way in the world. The remaining path will be concerned with this reversal process, as shown by comparing this card with the last of the major arcana.

When we turn around the 12, the number of The Hanged Man, we get 21 (see figure 29 on page 114). We know that the 21st card, as the end of the hero's journey, represents paradise regained; on another level it stands for the wholeness that has been achieved. If we compare the two cards with each other, the figure on the 21st card is seen

Figure 29. The Hanged Man and its reverse, The World. The 12 becomes 21, standstill turns into motion, and the upside-down world becomes the real world.

as the reversed Hanged Man. On it, the crossed legs are below while the open arm position above them indicates the triangle. The standstill of The Hanged Man becomes the living, dancing motion of the 21st card. In this way, the path is found out of the upside-down world into the real world.

As we will see, The Hanged Man signifies hopelessness in the face of Death—the following card—and the necessity of a confrontation with this unavoidable fate. As long as we turn our eyes away from it and try to suppress every thought of it as much as possible, we remain in the state of The Hanged Man, and will sooner or later become one of the (still) living dead. Yet, the path of initiation that begins here allows us to become truly liberated and living people, people who live with death, through the experiences of the following card. No one is free, said Martin Luther King, as long as he fears death.

The Hanged Man represents all the crises that want to force us to change our ways, and therefore also the central crises in the middle of life—the midlife crisis. This modern phrase may quickly awaken the impression of being an invention of the 20th century, but this is far from the truth. This crisis at the turning point in life, as we could more aptly call it, has always been a familiar one. Even Dante began his *Divine Comedy* with it: "Midway in our life journey, I went

Dante, who has lost his way in the woods; the beginning of The Divine Comedy ("The Forest," woodcut by Gustave Doré).

astray from the straight road and woke to find myself alone in a dark wood"[1] states the first sentence of this magnificent portrayal of a nighttime sea journey.

There can be no better description of what this card is about. Everything is in order; we believe we have it all firmly under control, and now this! This is how most tales of woe begin. We always believe we have everything under control. But that is neither the living present nor the future. At best, we can have the past and the many ideas that we have about reality and the future, in which we believe, under control. But to our annoyance, time and again life takes the freedom to develop in a totally different way than we have imagined or planned so wonderfully. This deeply indignant: ". . . and then this!" shows how unexpectedly we are surprised by the turning point in life (and other crises). To this effect, C. G. Jung commented that, "Even intelligent and cultivated people live their lives without even knowing of the possibility of such transformations. Wholly unprepared, they embark upon the second half of life." In his opinion, there should be "schools for forty-year olds" to prepare them for their coming life and its demands. These did not appear to be necessary in earlier times when religions were strong enough to offer comprehensive help covering all the stages of life."[2]

But this is not meant to say that the significance of this card is limited to the midlife crisis. It naturally stands for all the crises in which we are stuck, which become trials of patience and force a change of attitude or a change of direction. The impression should also not arise that these crises can be avoided with smartness, piety, or behaving like a model student. "Nobody who finds himself on the road to wholeness," says C. G. Jung, as if he were describing this card, "can escape that characteristic suspension which is the meaning of crucifixion. For he will infallibly run into things that thwart and cross him: first, the thing he has no wish to be (the shadow); second, the thing he is not (the 'other,' the individual reality of the 'You'); and third, his psychic non-ego (the collective unconscious)." And somewhat later he adds: "The meeting with the collective unconscious is a fatality of which the natural man has no inkling until it overtakes him."[3]

This crisis is often triggered by one of the primal fears, which Karlfried Graf Dürckheim describes as the threefold plight of all

---

[1] Dante, *The Divine Comedy*, "Inferno," 1.1.
[2] C. G. Jung, "The Stages of Life," in *The Structure and Dynamics of the Psyche*, CW, vol. 8, ¶ 784.
[3] C. G. Jung, "Psychology of the Transference," in *The Practice of Psychotherapy*, CW, vol. 16, ¶ 470.

human beings[4]: the fear of destruction (death or ruin), the fear of desolate loneliness, or the fear of despairing at the question of meaning in life. Above all, this last fear is particularly insidious because very few people expect it. Yet, at the same time, it is a sense of meaning in particular that lets us remain upright during even the worst crises, whereby even small crises can be experienced as unbearable when they appear meaningless and absurd to us.

But particularly here, toward the end of the second of the three sections of the path, the course of which has been concerned with the development of the ego, the greatest crisis of meaning is often waiting. And everything was going so well up to now. We have developed a healthy ego and achieved all of its significant goals: a car, a home, success, an impressive bank account, a great husband/a wonderful wife, and a happy family. We enjoy prestige, feel ourselves to be very important, and are actually in good shape. We think! Perhaps we even have turned the dream of life "on the island" into reality and seriously believed that we could "drop out." But suddenly, we are forced to discover with dismay that we are stuck in the middle of it all and there is no dropping out. All of a sudden, we notice how stale everything tastes. We try to anesthetize ourselves or try to reproduce the old thrill with increasingly higher dosages. But the certainty that nothing helps dawns on us with increasing vehemence. Now, when we actually have everything, we are suddenly completely empty and see with horror that there is actually only death waiting for us. How terrifying! And the problem gets worse and worse because we believe we can continue to solve new problems with old, apparently proven answers. "But we cannot live the afternoon of life according to the programme of life's morning," C. G. Jung points out, "for what was great in the morning will be little at evening, and what in the morning was true will at evening have become a lie."[5]

The consciousness researcher Ken Wilber also describes the background of this crisis in a very emphatic manner: "We have identified ourselves with our body, mind, and personality, imagining these objects to constitute our real 'self,' and we then spend our entire lives trying to defend, protect, and prolong what is just an illusion."[6] But, he also relates how valuable these crises are: "Contrary to most professional opinion, this gnawing dissatisfaction with life is not a

---

[4] Cf. Karlfried Graf Dürckheim, *Meditieren—wozu und wie* (Frieburg, Germany: Herder, 1976), p. 36.
[5] C. G. Jung, "The Stages of Life," CW, vol. 8, ¶ 784.
[6] Ken Wilber, *No Boundary* (Boston: Shambhala, 1981), p. 57.

Figure 30. The Hanged Man in the Tarot of Marseilles; he hangs by the left leg. The Hanged Man in the Waite Tarot; he hangs by the right leg.

sign of 'mental illness,' nor an indication of poor social adjustment, nor a character disorder. For concealed within this basic unhappiness with life and existence is the embryo of a growing intelligence, a special intelligence usually buried under the immense weight of social shams." Suffering wants to help this special intelligence achieve a breakthrough, which is why people either avoid, scorn, or fail to become aware of it. But, to the same extent, we should not glorify suffering, cling to it, or dramatize it, but should use it as the impetus for perception.

Since situations of this type usually grab hold of us on the left side, meaning the unconscious side, The Hanged Man is depicted on the older tarot cards as hanging by his left leg. Waite was the first person to change this symbolism in order to make it clear that there can be good reasons for consciously (right side) assuming this position.

The Hanged Man always means that we have reached the end of a path and must turn around, that we are also looking at something the wrong way and must change our way of thinking, that a matter stagnated because we have overlooked or forgotten something important. And, in addition to the sincere willingness to change our way of thinking, we need patience—a great deal of patience. This card is also frequently interpreted to mean a sacrifice, since the crisis it represents usually demands that we give up the familiar posture, an expectation that has been self-evident up to now, or a perspective that has become

Figure 31. The Empress shows development and growth in outer abundance. The Hanged Man symbolizes root formation and growth into the depths.

a foregone conclusion, so that life can continue. With this background, Waite's changed portrayal challenges us to not wait until fate forces us to alter our direction, but consciously take this position time and again so that, as a result of the completely changed perspective of the headstand, we will receive valuable insights. This is why the head of The Hanged Man is surrounded by a halo, a sign that he has seen the light (figure 30). The goal of this card is also the formation of roots and growth into the depths, a meaning that is complemented by The Empress, with which it is connected through its cross sum. She, in turn, represents growth in outer abundance (figure 31).

On a deeper level, this card stands for a person who voluntarily makes a sacrifice. The form of the T-cross refers to the Greek letter Tau (T), whose Hebraic equivalent Thau (ת) resembles the supporting framework on the card in the Marseilles Tarot. However, in biblical times the Hebraic character still had the same form as the Greek letter[7] and was considered the sign of the chosen one. It was the mark of Cain that, in contrast to popular belief, was not a stigma, but the sign of someone who God had put under his special protection (Genesis 4:15). Among the Israelites up to the time of the judges, it was tattooed onto the foreheads of the tribal members as a royal caste dis-

---

[7] Cf. Robert Graves, *The White Goddess* (London: Faber, 1977), p. 210.

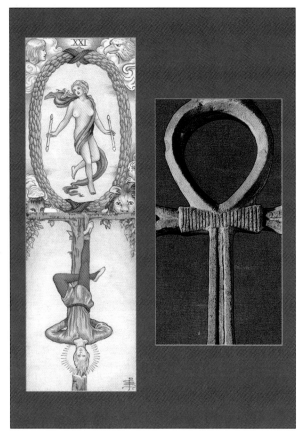

Figure 32. Combined, The World and The Hanged Man form the ankh.

tinction. From their ranks, they chose the holy king, who sacrificed himself at the end of his term of office.

Combined, cards XII and XXI, The Hanged Man and The World, result in the ankh, the ancient Egyptian loop cross consisting of a circle and a staff (see figure 32). In the unification of these symbols for the feminine and the masculine gender, the Egyptians saw the sign of life.

The biggest task that faces us is moving from The Hanged Man to The World and uniting these two poles. Bound to the earthly cross (The Hanged Man), we sense a deep longing for paradise (The World). Something within us hears the call of the self, which wants to lead our ego to wholeness—and to the highest level of unity of all things. Whether a person follows this call, whether he walks through this doorway to initiation,

remains to be seen. And even if he does this, there is no guarantee that he will ever reach the goal. Yet, he is also free to continue to let himself "hang." The "obligatory section" of the journey ends with the next card, Death. It is very certain that all of us, without exception, will reach this point. But whether the path ends here or continues on, leading to the Highest, depends upon each individual alone. The self, whose attainment is the goal in life, is—as Emma Jung emphasizes— "not complete, but is present in us as a potentiality which can become manifest only in the course of a specific processes." However, there is no guarantee that the self will be "realized through the unfolding of the natural biological life process. There appear to be many lives where this does not come to pass."[8]

---

8 Emma Jung and Marie-Louise von Franz, *The Grail Legend* (New York: Putnam, 1970), p. 133.

Keywords for THE HANGED MAN

ARCHETYPE:	The test
TASK:	Changing one's ways, insight and willingness to make a sacrifice
GOAL:	Growth into the depths
RISK:	Letting oneself hang, endlessly turning in circles
FEELING IN LIFE:	Being hopelessly stuck on a treadmill or in the wrong place, life crises, getting in one's own way, meaningless lack of activity, wearing down, exercise in humility, testing one's patience

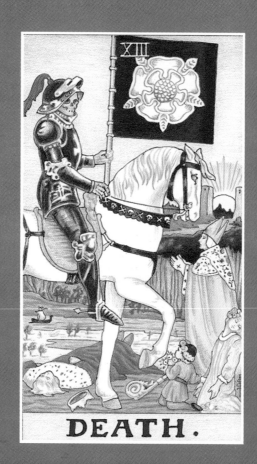

 n a Zen story, the master warns his dying student: "Dying is an interesting experience, but fearfulness will spoil this experience for you."[1] The same applies to Death, one of the most feared tarot cards—and, at the same time, one of the most misunderstood. It represents the natural end, a force that has exhausted itself and therefore must regenerate. In any case, this card means that one phase has come to an end and it is time to say farewell. On the other hand, it does not say whether this parting is something we have feared or whether we may have possibly yearned for and expected it for some time.

The people on the card either look or walk to the left. The left is west, sunset, darkness, the end, and night. In comparison, Death itself rides to the right,

Death
Descent into the Underworld

to the east, to the new morning. This is also the direction of the wind and the direction in which the Pharaoh's death-boat, which can be seen on the river, is headed. In the east, we can see the immortal sun behind the simple towers, the heralds of the heavenly Jerusalem that we will encounter again on the 18th card. Through this change of direction, the card illustrates that in such phases we human beings only see the dark side of things. We only have doom, the end, and absolute nothingness before our eyes. The actual meaning of this experience is found by going through a profound process of transformation to a new morning and a new liveliness.

This observation should not encourage us, in apparent enlightenment, to interpret the Death card as the beginning of something new, prematurely leaving out the night that lies between the evening and the morning in the process. Death means departure and the conclusion of something. And only when this leave-taking has actually been completed, when the old has truly faded away, will the preconditions for the transformation exist. Hermann Weidelener[2], a German teacher, makes clear the true meaning of leave-taking when he challenges us to

---

[1] Janwillem van de Wetering, *Zen Koan as a Means of Realizing Enlightenment* (Boston: Tuttle, 1994).
[2] Herman Weidelener, *Die Goetter in uns* (Munich: Goldman, 1987), p. 68.

Figure 33. Without genuine separation, if we don't really finalize an ending, we will fall back into the state of The Hanged Man.

always ask whether we have fulfilled what a place has demanded from us before we leave it. Only in the consciousness of fulfillment can we go on our way with dignity. If we have failed to fulfill this, our leaving is merely flight. Instead, we tend to hurry from one place to the next, always driven by the hope of finding something better, more exciting, or more enjoyable there. We quickly tear open one door after the other without closing the old doors behind us, let alone considering the question of fulfillment. We constantly flee from actually "taking leave," and there is a curse in this flight. However, the challenge at this point is truly letting go as an indispensable precondition for something that is really new to come about. Truly letting go means letting go with our entire attention. The solution that saves us from the hopelessness of the previous card, The Hanged Man, always has as its prerequisite that we can first let go of the old without already having one eye on the new. Without a genuine separation, there is no true change. Instead, time and time again we fall into the previous situation of The Hanged Man and oscillate back and forth between these two cards.

This state can easily be compared with a scratch on a record, because of which we constantly have the same piece played to us. Whenever we have the feeling that we are stuck in such a "broken record" and have the same experience over and over, we can safely say that we are playing The Hanged Man and are avoiding Death (see figure 33). Typical equivalents for this are all the situations that allow us to get in our own way, where we avoid important developmental steps too many times. Strictly speaking, whether we lack confidence, if we are shy, afraid of failing, afraid of making fools of ourselves, or whether we think we are too good to take the step, actually makes no essential difference. In the first case, our ego is too weak and in the latter, it is inflated. But, any of these cases—even being shy—indicates that we take ourselves much too seriously and stand in our own way. The *Tao Te Ching* says of this situation:

> *A man on tiptoe cannot stand firm;*
> *A man astride cannot walk on;*
> *A man who displays himself cannot shine;*
> *A man who approves of himself cannot be noted;*
> *A man who praises himself cannot have merit;*
> *A man who glories in himself cannot excel;*
> *These, when compared with Tao, are called:*
> *"Excess in food and overdoing in action."*
> *Even in other things, mostly, they are rejected.*
> *Therefore the man of Tao does not stay with them.*[3]

This is why it is important to overcome the ego. This is why we must learn to not take ourselves so seriously and to push aside our ego (that we worked so hard to develop) so that the path to further development becomes unblocked.

Such a glitch is also a central motif in the wonderful hero's journey written about Bastian Balthasar Bux. A small, fat little boy, he sits on the roof of the schoolhouse and reads the book *The Neverending Story*. And the longer Bastian reads, the deeper he is drawn into the story. (The longer we read the book of our life, the deeper it will draw us into life.) And suddenly, the story asks him to jump into it because it cannot continue without him. But Bastian is not courageous enough and recoils from it. So the story immediately snaps back to its beginning and is told anew, time and again, until the point where he would have to jump into it. And finally, he has enough courage to do it. Bastian jumps into Fantasia, the underworld of *The Neverending Story*, and then the plot can continue.

The hamster on the wheel is another image that serves to illustrate running in place, which The Hanged Man symbolizes so well. Because of the desire, joy in life, and élan of the card Strength, we begin some actions that suddenly become a senseless rotation on their

---

[3] Lao Tzu, *Tao te Ching*, Ch'u Ta-kao, trans. (London: Allen & Unwin, 1917), verse 24.

own (The Hanged Man). However, we do not comprehend what has happened and why the thing that previously gave us so much joy and that let us sparkle with energy has suddenly become this running in place. Instead of looking for a genuine solution, such as leaving the wheel sideways, we attempt to do things according to the highly dubious method that Paul Watzlawick has described as "more of the same."[4] We increase our speed more and more, rushing on in the wheel of madness. Then, when an external power (Death) suddenly stops the wheel, we are naturally quite perplexed at first, just as the hamster would be. Completely at a loss, we try to get the wheel running a few more times before we leave it with a heavy heart in the firm conviction that everything is now over. But stepping back, we may perhaps recognize the absurdity of the whole thing, and suddenly comprehend that we have enslaved ourselves in a futile situation. Only from this distance do we understand how much death has not only brought us the solution, but also true redemption.

The Hanged Man also corresponds to a piece of fruit on a tree that has become ripe and now must let itself fall in order to produce new life and new fruit. It experiences this act of letting itself fall as death. If it refuses to let go, it remains hanging on the tree and will gradually rot there without having produced new life. Yet, it also cannot prevent its end by doing this; it only becomes fruitless.

Translated to human beings, this image means that no one forces us to learn from our crises. If we experience The Hanged Man as something like our midlife crisis, it can also definitely stand for the entire second half of life. If we fail to seek or find an answer for the crisis around this turn of life other than by lamenting, complaining, and whining, we can easily spend the rest of our life doing it. In this case, death will one day mean the end of the journey and, at the same time, the end of life. But we also have the possibility of learning from these crises, letting go, and experiencing death as a central theme at midlife, after which the essential things follow. This is the reason why the tarot shows the Death card at the midpoint of the path and not at its end.

This approach is similar to the worldview of ancient cultures, such as that of the Celts, about whose Druids the Roman poet Lucan said: "If your songs contain truths, then death is just the middle of a long lasting existence."[5] Within this context, we can also understand the message: "If you die before you die, you will not die when you die." For this reason, sages of various nations have pointed out that the

[4] Cf. Paul Watzlawick, *Vom Schlecten des Guten* (Munich: Piper, 1991), p. 23.
[5] Lancelot Lengyel, *Le Secret des Celts* (Forcalquier, France: Robert Morel Editeur, 1969), p. 24.

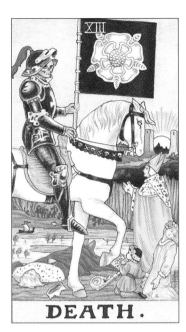

Figure 34. "Dying" and "Becoming" are opposites in the same polarity.

encounter and confrontation with death is a central theme of life. They have emphasized that the human being must die and be born again in order to be able to perceive reality. When it says in the Bible: "Teach us how short our life is so that we may become wise" (Psalms 90:12), then our ego would much rather understand this the other way around as: "Teach us to be so wise that we believe we must no longer die!"

In all of this, we should not forget that far-reaching changes need time. This concerns the descent into the underworld. The return to the light, the birth of something new, does not follow until six cards later with the 19th card, The Sun. These cards correspond to each other like evening and morning.

We see a light-colored horse on both cards. On Death, it is the fourth horse from the Apocalypse (Revelations 6:8), the pale horse upon which death rides. By way of contrast, The Sun shows us the white horse, the royal horse that carries the reborn hero. On the Death card, the sun is setting,[6] while it once again shines at full power on The Sun card. On Death, the horse is ridden by a skeleton; a child rides on The Sun card. (Because of this transformation, we can assume that there is a fountain of youth between these two cards;

---

[6] The setting sun corresponds with the theme of the card. Other commentaries on this interpret it as the rising sun. Although the sun on the east side would stand for this, the card itself does not represent the new morning. In any case, the sun is on the horizon, in contrast to its position at midday on The Sun card.

Figure 35. The descent into the underworld, or the hero's night sea journey.

otherwise, this remarkable rejuvenation cannot be explained. We find it on card XVII.) The child waves a red scarf, the color of life; whereas Death carries the black banner of death. However, its mystic white rose as a symbol of life is an indication of the life-renewing phase that Death introduces. The feather on the helmet of Death hangs down limply, but the feather on the head of the child stands erect. All this shows how much these two cards are linked with each other and that they represent the polarities of dying and becoming (see figure 34 on page 127). They stand for the descent into the underworld and the return to the light (The Sun). The night journey lies between them.

Cards XIII to XVIII are also called the night cards (see figure 35). They have either black motifs, like Death, The Devil, and The Tower, or symbols of the night, like The Moon and The Star. Only the card Temperance appears at first glance to be somewhat out of place in this dark company. But we will soon get to know it as an indispensable force in the underworld. It corresponds to the guide of souls, about which the books of death in the various cultures report. And since angels are the guides of souls in our Christian-Western tradition, the card shows an angel.

The motif of the journey to the other world, the sea journey at night, is not only familiar in all the religious traditions of the nations of both East and West, but also agrees without exception on each of the essential points. All of these cultures "consider death as a journey with the goal of once again achieving one's own unadulterated core of being, even if these journeys temporarily lead to Heaven and Hell or to the return in a new body; there is also agreement that only the wise person has a consciousness of death and that it is necessary to morally, spiritually, and imaginatively prepare for death—if a person wants to die in a good way."[7]

---

7 Carol Zaleski, *Otherworld Journeys* (New York and London: Oxford University Press, 1988), p. 40.

The soul bird Ba rises up from the body of the deceased (Papyrus of Ani, British Museum, London).

Nut, the Goddess of the Sky (Egyptian Museum, Cairo).

In order to discover what the night sea journey is about, we can look at the underworld of the Egyptians, since no other people have handed down so many impressive images of what their sages have seen in the other worlds. There we see how the soul rises up from the body of the deceased. It is called Ba and is depicted by a bird that subsequently goes on the journey.

The deceased is guarded by protective deities like Nut, the Goddess of the Sky, or the scorpion goddess Selket, while the jackal-headed Anubis or the wolf-headed Wepwawet accompanies his "Ba" as guides of the soul on the further path through the other world to Maat, the Goddess of Justice.

Maat is always depicted with an ostrich feather, as shown in the plate on page 130. Even the ostrich feather, alone, is considered to be a sign for the presence of divine justice. The decisive test, the Court of the Dead, takes place in the hall named after the goddess, the Hall of Maat.

The papyrus on page 130 shows Anubis (left) accompanying the deceased into the hall as the soul guide. In one pan of the scale, there is a vessel with the heart of the deceased; in the other pan, there is a feather, the symbol of Maat, the symbol of incorruptible, absolute justice. At the head of the scale, her sign can be seen as well. Anubis reads the result from the pointer and tells it to the record-keeper, who stands to the

The scorpion goddess, Selket (Egyptian Museum, Cairo).

right. It is the ibis-headed Thoth, the Egyptian God of Wisdom, as the record-keeper of the underworld who writes down the result. If the heart of the deceased is just as heavy as the feather, then the pointer of the scale will stand as straight as a plumb line, and the deceased is in order. Then he has lived in the right way and is allowed to go to Osiris, the lord of the realm of the dead.

If his heart is too light or too heavy, then he has fallen short, and is lost. This is precisely what the monster next to the scale is waiting for. The glutton, as the Egyptians called it, was then permitted to devour the heart forever. In the depicted scene, the deceased has passed the test. This is why Horus is leading him to Osiris, behind whose throne Isis and Nephtys are also standing and welcome him. He will remain in the realm of Osiris until Anubis comes to blow the breath of life into him through the ritual of opening the mouth, so that he can once again return to the upper world.

Above: Maat, the Goddess of Justice (Museo Archeologico, Florence).
Below: The weighing of the heart in the Hall of Maat (Papyrus of Hunefer, British Museum, London).

So the scale as the symbol of balance is a central theme in the Egyptian underworld. We find the tarot equivalent in the balance of the card Temperance. However, the corresponding room of this underworld journey is the Hall of Maat, the Goddess of Justice, whose sign is the feather. In the cards of the major arcana, only three figures wear a feather on the head: The Fool, Death, and the child on The Sun card.

These three cards are connected with each other on several levels (see figure 36, page 132). For one thing, The Fool is the hero who must descend into the underworld at Death, and who once again sees the light of day at The Sun. The feather is an indication of the tests that lie between, which correspond with the occurrences in the Hall of Maat. Another connection between The Fool and The Sun is found in the two figures that are similar to each other and yet completely different: the childlike fool and the wise fool, the naive fool and the pure fool. Between them lies Death as an unavoidable precondition for this fundamental transformation. In the same manner, the naive white sun on The Fool card finds its significant counterpole

Anubis performs the ritual of opening the mouth (Egyptian grave painting in Thebes).

through the encounter with Death (its alchemical blackening) and can therefore shine on The Sun card in immortal gold.

Above all, our Judaeo-Christian tradition knows the nighttime sea journey from the biblical story of Jonah, who was swallowed by the whale (Jonah 1–3). At the beginning, Jonah received the order from God: "Go to Neneveh, that great city and speak out against it"[which means: threaten them with punishment] (Jonah 1:2). As his task, this command corresponds with The Wheel of Fortune. What does Jonah do? He does what we all would most like to do as soon as we come into contact with one aspect of our task in life for the first time. He runs away.

At first, we would like to imagine this task to be something exalted, significant, and delightful. Some people are full of longing as they think: "Ah, if I just knew what my true task in life is," especially since they like to assume that it is somewhere in the realm of their talents

Figure 36. Three cards are connected with each other by the feather.

and strengths. But the task is always to become whole, and to do this we have no choice but to become involved with our opposite pole, with the inferior, primitive, sticky, awkward side that we have overlooked and often scorned up to now (see page 90ff.). But once we encounter the themes that are related to it, we are immediately indignant and reject them with an angry: "Anything! But not that!" It can almost be said that whenever we exclaim this, "Anything! But not that!" from the depths of our soul, we have with a high degree of certainty encountered a mosaic stone of our life task.

So Jonah probably also thought: "Me? Go to Nineveh? I'm not crazy! They'll certainly kill me there. Anything! But not that!" So instead, he boards a ship to travel in exactly the opposite direction, to Greece. The Greeks called such a refusal to follow the divine command *hubris*, which means "self-conceit" and "insolent defiance." As we have seen in the 11th card, such a sacrilege lies in the spectrum of meaning related to the card Strength. According to the Greek view, it is primarily this offense that the gods immediately punish, and so even Jonah does not have to wait long for recompense in the form of The Hanged Man.

Is there a more hopeless trap than a ship in distress at sea? This is exactly what happens to Jonah. Completely at a loss and stricken with fear, the sailors cast lots to find out who is to blame for this calamity. It falls on Jonah, who immediately shows himself to be repentant, sincerely confesses, and assumes the blame for the calamity. Because he has evaded God's command, he is willing to die; so, after some hesitation, the sailors throw him overboard. But instead of dying in the waves as he had expected, he is swallowed by a fish. He spends three days and three nights (a typical time period for the nighttime sea journey) in its belly before the animal spits him out on land. After this period of purification, Jonah is ready to accept God's command and fulfill his task in life.

On the basis of the tarot cards, this story can be retold quite well. But since the Bible only tells us the prayer that Jonah says in the belly of the fish and not what he experienced there, we find no correlations with cards XIV to XVIII (see figure 37 on page 134).

Jonah, who was swallowed by the whale: a typical motif of a night sea journey (Cappella degli Scrovegni all'Arena, Padua).

With card XIII, we have reached the end of the second third of the path, the course that deals with developing and overcoming the ego, thereby subjecting it to the higher self. "Whenever the conscious and the animal personality is in conflict with the inner process of growth, it suffers crucifixion," says Marie-Louise von Franz, as if she were describing The Hanged Man. "The self-will of the conscious personality has to die and surrender to the process of inner growth."[8] This is why this stage means overcoming the ego, not an "egocide," but the "murder" of the ego, so to speak.

---

[8] Marie-Louise von Franz, *Shadow and Evil in Fairy Tales* (Zurich: Spring, 1974), pp. 39–40.

Figure 37. God's command (Wheel of Fortune); hubris (Strength); ship in distress (The Hanged Man); thrown overboard (Death); protection and guidance (Temperance); return to land (The Sun).

The Hanged Man makes us weary and ready for this purpose. But this observation should not lead to the premature conclusion that the ego forces will no longer play a role on the future path. In the positive sense, they place themselves in the service of the self, the symbol of the greater whole. However, they can also regroup in a questionable, excessively power-hungry manner, and can therefore halt the transformation process at any time.

The tarot cards link The Emperor and Death with each other through the cross sum and thereby show the interaction between these two principles (figure 38). While The Emperor builds structures, and raises the foundation walls of ego feeling in the process, this card is concerned with dissolving and overcoming it. The ego constantly sets limits, boundaries between ego and non-ego, between ego and shadow, between mind and body, between God and human being, between good and evil, and so forth. At this point we must, or should, once again recognize how false all boundaries ultimately are. They originally had their value, their function, and their justification, since they served to build the ego, which had to separate itself from the rest in order to come into existence. And yet, all boundaries are wrong and arbitrary.[9] This is why they should not become lasting. Whenever we come to this place on the path, we must dissolve and overcome the boundaries in order to make room for our increasingly expanding experience. The Hanged Man makes us weary until we are willing to make the sacrifice of overcoming these boundaries.

In the connection that the two cards have with each other, there is an additional message. At this point on the journey, we have finally reached the limits of the feasible (The Emperor = action and power). After this, nothing more can be forced—just as we cannot fall asleep at will, or force ourselves to do so, nor can we monitor or observe our-

---

[9] Cf. Ken Wilber, *No Boundary* (Boston: Shambhala, 1981).

Figure 38. Building structures (The Emperor); the
end of structure (Death).

selves falling asleep. All of these are the ego's attempts at controlling the situation; however, it must fail at this threshold. We can only create the preconditions of practicing the art of letting things happen and—as in sleep—trust that we will pass over into the other state.

Since ancient times, the human being has feared everything hostile to life, and glorified even more whatever intensifies life. Thanatos, meaning death, and Eros, as the life force, are the representatives of these two poles in the Greek world of myth.[10] Even the most ancient magic always attempted to ban the death pole and conjure up the life pole. Today we do the same thing by passing over the theme of death in silence, and putting it under a taboo, while we glorify everything that intensifies life in film and television, in advertising and consumer frenzy, in the body cult and the worship of eternal youth. Within the cards of the major arcana, these opposites are found in Strength and Death; between them lies The Hanged Man, in as far as Strength is kept in its original 11th position.

The human being is crucified (The Hanged Man) between the polarities—death (Death) and life (Strength). See figure 39, page 136. With increasing age, the ego becomes more frequently aware of its ephemerality and inescapability in the face of death. In its despair, it

---

[10] Eros, which is equated with Strength here and not with The Lovers, must be understood in its original form as the primal force, just as the most ancient Greek traditions still described him as the God of Creation. Only many centuries later did he become the arrow-shooting Cupid boy.

Figure 39. Eros (Strength XI) and Thanatos (Death XIII), the life polarity and the death polarity between which the human being is crucified (The Hanged Man XII), from the Tarot of Marseilles.

attempts to conjure up the life polarity in order to distract itself from the unavoidable fate. "Each of us is a worthy object of complaint," says Elias Canetti to this effect. "Each of us is stubbornly convinced that he should not die."[11]

Through a program of activity, through sports, sexuality, and amusements of all types, we strive to experience pleasure, and constantly prove to ourselves anew our unbroken liveliness in order to avoid—as much as possible—the glance in the other direction, the look into nothingness, of which the ego is terrified.

Quick therapies are very popular today, for they seduce their patients into believing in quick cures, and boast of their success and apparent superiority to the transpersonal therapy methods that take longer but are more profound. Many of these rapid methods motivate the emotionally depressed person to do something exciting. When such a spark ignites the inner fire, the individual will actually feel good for a while. However, as the tarot cards show, the path from The Hanged Man to Strength is a step backward. This is why a greater dose of Strength is required each time to conjure up the life polarity because the certainty of death knocks with increasing vehemence on the doors of consciousness. Sooner or later, life will force us in an inevitable and inexorable way to continue in the other direction and look into the eyes of the unavoidable, for we cannot avoid looking at death and transience.

---

[11] Elias Canetti, *Crowds and Power* (Noonday Press, 1984), p. 526.

Death shows the direction (©Salvadore Dali, Der Todesreiter, 1935/©Demart pro Arte B.V./VG Bild-Kunst, Bonn, 1999; used by permission).

In this process, it does not matter how clever, well-conceived, or extensive our concepts of Death are. The only decisive factor is how we approach it, how close we let this experience get to us, and how deeply we are touched by it.

Just as a cathedral remains a dead museum as long as we only tour it, we cannot sense the meaning of death as long as we just think about it. But as soon as we kneel down, we change from being the observer to the person who prays, from the onlooker to the person who devoutly belongs to it. In this same moment, the museum turns into a temple and cold, hostile death becomes a holy experience.

The more honest we are in getting down on our knees, the more enriching will be the experience we have in the process. On the one hand, this is because our reverence for life grows in the closeness to death; on the other hand, because death is the actual initiation, the only doorway to what is truly secret. Everything that has been called secret on the path already covered was just mystery-mongering in comparison to this.

The more we turn our eyes away with a dogged and fear-filled attitude, the more hectic and extreme the to and fro between the good mood and the bad mood becomes. In its extreme form, this refusal leads to manic-depressive symptoms. The more manically the life polarity (Strength) is conjured up, the deeper the following respective plunge into depression (The Hanged Man) will be. Death shows us the solution. It shows us the right direction.

In his great work on the development of the human mind, Ken Wilber makes it clear that true transformations can only take place through Thanatos, the death pole. Eros, the life polarity, can only provide changes in the sense of diversion.[12] He compares consciousness with an eight-storey house. Once the ego has made itself comfortably at home on one of the floors and has gotten used to the view, it would actually like to remain there and not move onto any other floor. But if life there begins to be insipid, empty, and disconsolate, or if melancholy phases occur in the face of this monotony, then the ego quickly conjures up the life polarity and provides for some diversity. This means that we rearrange the furniture but stay within the same walls. In other words, we look for a new job, start a new relationship, look for some excitement in sex and play, once again give in to a shopping urge, or do whatever promises us a change of pace in our outer life

---

[12] Cf. Ken Wilber, *Up from Eden* (Wheaton, IL: Theosophical, 1996), p. 77ff..

without really becoming dangerous to our ego. Profound transformation can only take place through the death polarity, through which we leave our previous floor of consciousness. Only this contains the opportunity of penetrating through to superconsciousness. However, the price of any fundamental transformation includes the risk of crashing in the process. And precisely here is the danger connected with this stage and this card. On the journey through the night, the path of initiation that begins here, there is no guaranteed return ticket. But there are the guides of souls!

Keywords for DEATH	
ARCHETYPE:	Death
TASK:	Leave-taking and descent into the underworld, withdrawing, concluding something, separating
GOAL:	Separation, overcoming the ego, dissolving the boundaries, profound transformation
RISK:	Playing dead out of fear, crashing
FEELING IN LIFE:	Experiencing a conclusion, exhaustion—the search for peace and regeneration, experience of leave-taking

rying to understand it on the basis of its name hardly reveals the meaning of this card. Although temperance (moderation) is considered one of the cardinal virtues, this word has become so devalued in contemporary usage that people rarely associate positive values with "temperate" today. On the other hand, if we recognize the symbol of the right mixture in its motif, we will find the actual message of the card.

There has already been a great deal of speculation as to what the angel is mixing and whether it is mixing at all, or just pouring from one container into the other. The latter situation would express that the energies, which had flowed into outer growth up to now, are finally being poured in the opposite direction in order to produce inner growth from now on. This is certainly an essential statement of the

Temperance
The Guide of Souls

card. It is even more important to understand the right mixture as an expression of successful unification, an essential theme of this last section of the path. After death has dissolved the boundaries that the ego previously had to build, from now on it will be important to unify what had been separated before. However, the card also stands for proper moderation as an expression of a sensitivity that is imperative in order to survive the dangers lurking on the rest of the journey. The guide of souls, which the card shows us as an angel, symbolizes this infallible knowledge of the right path. In the Christian tradition, it is the Archangel Michael who assumes this task. Old portrayals show him in a motif that is quite reminiscent of the test in the Hall of Maat. A devil attempts to get the scale off balance, but Michael wards him off. This brings the scale (and the human being) back into balance.

Despite its light colors, this card shows an underworld motif. The image of the lilies is a key to this interpretation. According to Greek tradition, they grow in the underworld, which is why Hades was also called the Asphodeline ground (Asphodeline = type of lily). The iris not only bears the name Iris, the messenger of the gods, but it is also her symbol, and a sign of the presence of this Greek goddess, who was knowledgeable about the underworld. In Christian symbolism, the Easter lily is considered the passion flower. When we consider the stretch of the path upon which we find ourselves here, the parallel to

Michael, the weigher of souls (Guariento di Arpo, Museo Bottacin, Padua).

the Passiontide is obvious. The cards from The Hanged Man (XII) to The Devil (XV) show Christ's way of the Cross and the descent into the underworld. This is in harmony with the Christian creed, in which it says: "He was crucified, He died, and He was buried, and He descended into Hell . . ."; especially since the Bible reports of an angel at the grave (figure 40 on page 143).

The path that the cards show is a symbol of the narrow path of individuation, of becoming one's self. It leads (back) to the light, to the sun, which conceals a crown within itself. It can be seen in the dotted line, if the card is moved back and forth a bit. After the death of the old king (the ego), the path to the sun and to the crowning of the new king (the self) begins here. This is a motif that finds its equivalent in all the fairy tales where the hero becomes the king at the end of the story. So the path of ego development and overcoming the ego seen in cards VI to XII becomes the *actual self-experience* and *self-development* in the deepest sense of the word on this last third of the transpersonal section of the path.

The self, the force that brings order to what happens on the level of the soul and the emotions, wants to lead the human being to wholeness. This goal can be read in more than just the many dream motifs. On the playful level, this urge can be found in the impulse to finish a puzzle, to do a crossword, to play a game of solitaire, or in the desire to complete a collection. This inner force, which remains largely unconscious in everyday life, makes itself known in the way it urges us on to wholeness. While previous ego development meant separation from the whole, now it is the striving of the self that leads us on the path to unity, to wholeness. We must trust this previously unconscious guidance in order to do this, but the ego will resist because it is either too proud or too weak and fearful.

Figure 40. Crucified (The Hanged Man), died (Death), and buried (Temperance), and the descent into Hell (The Devil). This sequence of the Christian profession of faith is reflected in the tarot cards XII to XV.

In the first case, there is a lack of insight; in the second, there is a lack of trust. This is why the self often first makes sure that we entangle ourselves in a completely hopeless situation, in a life crisis. Here, the ego must fail because all the shrewdness, all the smartness, and even the cleverest tricks of our otherwise so intelligent and agile consciousness suddenly cannot help us any more. Consequently, helplessness, hopelessness, and abysmal resignation spread until the ego is at the end of its strength. Now the only possibility is letting go in complete desperation, firmly convinced that everything is over. But instead of—as expected—perishing or falling into the bottomless pit, to our great surprise we feel how we are carried by a power that is far greater than anything that we have ever known before and what has held us up to now. This surprising encounter with the self corresponds with the whale in the story of Jonah.

In a letter, C. G. Jung told how he personally had this experience because of a heart attack: "I was free, completely free and whole, as I had never felt before. . . . It was a silent, invisible festival and an incomparable, indescribable feeling of eternal bliss imbued it; never had I believed that such a feeling lay within the range of human experience. Seen from the outside, and as long as we are on the outside of death, it is the greatest cruelty. But as soon as you stand within it, you experience such a strong feeling of wholeness and peace and fulfillment that you no longer want to return."[1]

---

[1] C. G. Jung, *Letters,* vol. I (Princeton: Princeton University Press, 1974), letter dated Feb. 1, 1945 to K. Mann.

Figure 41. The "hope-
less" crisis (The Hanged
Man); failure and let-
ting go of the ego
(Death); the encounter
with the self
(Temperance).

C. G. Jung called this rare ability of the unconscious psyche to transform a person who is stuck in a hopeless situation and lead him into a new one the transcendental function. The Hanged Man, Death, and Temperance show us this transformation as the transition from the middle to the last third of the path (see figure 41).

In this last section of the path, many things are different, and some things that were foregone conclusions before and perceived objectively right now become invalid. This includes our experience of time, as well as our attitude toward death and our entire value system. As children, we experience time in cyclic terms. The year revolves around the celebration of Christmas. Sometimes it was far away, and then it got closer again. But it was always the same Christmas. Now that we are adults, we experience time in a linear, chronological fashion. Now one year follows the other. The cycle is broken, time has become a line with a beginning and an end. We experience time as a quantity, and therefore as limited. At first this does not matter much, since we live in the feeling of having an endless amount of time ahead of us. But by the middle of life at the latest, we notice how it is becoming increasingly fast and scarce. We figure out how much time we probably have left, try to hold onto it, make an effort to do many things at the same time in order to "save" time, live increasingly faster, more hectically, and then still must helplessly see how time mercilessly melts away.[2]

But when one is alone and it is night and so dark and still that one hears nothing and sees nothing but the thoughts which add and subtract the years, and the long row of those disagreeable facts which remorselessly indicate how far the hand of the clock

---

[2] The greater majority of all meaningful inventions of the technological age serve to save time. But oddly enough, people have less time today than ever.

has moved forward, and the slow, irresistible approach of the wall of darkness which will eventually engulf everything I love, possess, wish for, hope for, and strive for, then all our profundities about life slink off to some undiscoverable hiding-place, and fear envelops the sleepless one like a smothering blanket.[3]

But when we succeed in pressing forward to the last third of the path, we understand more and more that time does not necessarily mean the time on the clock, and it was wrong to measure it in amounts because its intensity alone is decisive. Time is not a quantity, but a quality. As a result, it is unimportant *how long* we live, but *how* we live; and not *how much* we experience but *how deeply*. With this background, a new attitude toward death also arises. It is no longer just the terrible end, after which everything is over. We should also not just seek the sanctimonious consolation of the ego, which, with all its means, hopes for reincarnation in the body. This may take place on Judgment Day or in the next incarnation.

Instead, we learn to comprehend ourselves as a part of the immortal whole, from which we were never separated, and in which we will rise again. Just as the wave never separates from the sea, our ego has never really been separated from the whole. And just as the wave must again become one with the ocean, our ego will dissolve and once again become one with the original source of all being. Each part of a wave has naturally already often been a part of many other waves before. But would it not be absurd for one wave to claim that it had already existed many times before? It sounds just as absurd and arrogant when the ego lays claim to already having lived many times (and naturally as a famous personality). This does not mean to say that the thought of reincarnation itself is farfetched. However, making it into a cheap anesthetic against the ego's fear of death appears to be highly questionable and diverts from a deeper understanding of the meaning of death. Instead, Ken Wilber advises: "Sacrifice self-immortality and discover the immortality of all Being." In another place, he says: "To move from subconsciousness to self-consciousness is to make death conscious; to move from self-consciousness to superconsciousness is to make death obsolete."[4] There appears to be much more truth in this than in all the contrived models for explaining away death.

In this sequence of the major arcana, it also becomes very clear what true creativity means. If we live in a largely unconscious manner

3 C. G. Jung, "The Soul and Death," in *The Structure and Dynamics of the Psyche,* CW, vol. 8, ¶ 796.
4 Cf. Ken Wilber, *Up from Eden* (Wheaton, IL: Theosophical, 1996), pp. 149, 360.

Figure 42. The ego trap (The Hanged Man); overcoming the ego (Death); surrender to higher guidance (Temperance); the potential of the depths (The Devil); bursting the old framework (The Tower); new hope, new horizons (The Star).

during the first third of life, we will develop ego consciousness during the middle section of the path. Although this is an essential precondition for every creative process, true creativity is also prevented by our ego consciousness to the degree in which it only wants to prove how wonderful it is. We can find this phenomenon in those who once had a good idea, who experienced or created something extremely impressive, and then proudly tell this same story over and over again for the rest of their lives. Such dead ends, in which nothing new is created, but things that have long been known are reproduced in a poorly repackaged version, correspond with The Hanged Man. The ego only repeats the perceptions from earlier times, which are about as exciting as the hundredth turn of the hamster wheel. True creativity can only be found on the last third of the path, which follows The Hanged Man. The precondition for it is withdrawing the ego. Only then can a higher force flow through us and lead us to new insights, statements, and courses of action.

The Death card symbolizes the threshold to this area. It stands for deep transformation, thanks to which the conscious mind no longer is dominated by an overly power-hungry ego. Instead, the ego that has become humble entrusts the self as a higher authority with the guidance.

Actual creative potential lies in the depths. Where else could it be than in the areas into which we have not yet looked? Whatever is on the surface and in the light has already long been monopolized by the ego. Only the insights into the dark, unconscious areas that have been avoided, blocked, or feared up to now extend beyond the previous scope. They can reveal new perspectives, new hopes, and new horizons. The tarot shows us all of this in the cards from The Hanged Man (XII) to The Star (XVII) (see figure 42).

Virgil leads Dante in the descent into the Inferno ("Geryon," woodcut by Gustave Doré).

The Cumaean Cybele leads Aeneas through the underworld [detail] (Jan Brueghel, the Elder, Kunsthistorisches Museum, Vienna; used by permission).

That this overcoming of the ego is the decisive step in the search for what is authentic, mysterious, and wonderful is also told by the following ancient Chinese story of the magic pearl:[5] The Lord of the Yellow Earth wandered beyond the boundary of the world. There he came to a very high mountain and watched the cycle of recurrence. And there he lost his magic pearl. He sent out knowledge to look for it, but did not get it back. He sent out keen-sightedness to look for it, but did not get it back. He sent out thought to look for it, but did not get it back. Then he sent out self-forgetfulness.[6] Self-forgetfulness found it. The Lord of the Yellow Earth spoke: "It is indeed strange that precisely self-forgetfulness was able to find it!"

On our journey, we approach the Inferno, the deepest and darkest point of our travels. Since things now go steeply downhill, and there are deep abysses to be traversed, unknown dangers and critical tightrope walks that must be crossed through, the hero would be hopelessly lost without an experienced guide.

But where and how can we find a soul guide? It would be futile to look for one since there is nothing to be done here on the feminine stretch of the path; here we can only let things happen. But being open and ready for it attracts the guide. Strictly speaking, it was always there but we just overlooked and overheard it. As an archetype, the soul guide

---

[5] Chuang Tsu, *Das wahre Buch vom südlichen Blütenland* (Munich: Diederichs, 1969).
[6] When we differentiate between the ego and the self in the Jungian sense, then ego-forgetfulness should certainly be used here. Ego-forgetfulness can be the positive counterpole to the saying, "I forgot myself!"

is obviously an inner authority, even if we like to project it onto other people, such as a therapist, priest, friend, muse, or guru. As the myths teach us, this is almost always a person of the opposite sex. In this manner, Perseus was guided by Athene and Theseus by Ariadne. The glorious Odysseus owes it to Circe that he became neither a victim of the dangerous Sirens nor the monsters Scylla and Charybdis. Aeneas lets himself be led through the underworld by the Cumaean Cybele and Heracles' follows Athene's advice. Psyche would have remained unconscious in the underworld without her connection to Amor. For Dante, first it was Virgil who led him through the depths of the Inferno to the Mount of Purgatory. However, this happened at the express request of Beatrice, Dante's actual soul guide, who then guided him on the further path to Paradise and the view of the Highest.

Seen in psychological terms, the soul guide is our own inner opposite sexuality—the anima or animus. Those who entrust themselves to the initially unconscious force will certainly be guided better than those who listen to the cleverest of advice from other people. At the same time, it is helpful to carry on a true dialog with one's anima or animus. Even if at the beginning it feels quite strange to talk to "one's self" out loud, thanks to Jungian psychology it is sufficiently known how productive such conversations can soon become. Jung emphasized that he really meant this to be a technique and said of it: "The art of it consists only in allowing our invisible partner to make herself heard, in putting the mechanism of expression momentarily at her disposal, without being overcome by the distaste one naturally feels at playing such an apparently ludicrous game with oneself, or by doubts as to the genuineness of the voice of one's interlocutor."[7] He goes on to explain that we believe, at least at the beginning, that we have made up all the answers that come because we like to believe that we "make" our own thoughts. But they are just as intentional or voluntary as a dream, particularly when they are formulated for affect. In order to not become victims of our own "humbug," he admonishes in closing: "Scrupulous honesty with oneself and no rash anticipation of what the other side might conceivably say are the indispensable conditions of this technique for educating the anima."[8] Through these dialogs, the consciousness' willingness to consider the images and messages of the unconscious mind and include them in everyday life increases more and more.

---

[7] C. G. Jung, "The Relation between the Ego and the Unconscious," in *Two Essays on Analytical Psychology*, CW, vol. 7, ¶ 323.
[8] C. G. Jung, "The Relation between the Ego and the Unconscious," CW, vol. 7, ¶ 323.

Figure 43. Renunciation and abstinence (Death); the proper mixture (Temperance); excess, greed, and dependence (The Devil).

If we consider the dark neighborhood of Temperance, we can see that it has nothing to do with mediocrity, halfheartedness, innocuousness, or pale hypocrisy. The tarot places it between Death and The Devil (see figure 43). The relationship to The Devil is easy to comprehend. One of the latter's meanings is excess in contrast to Temperance, which represents moderation. So the juxtaposition of these cards is a mirror of many developments that often begin in the proper proportion, but sooner or later degenerate into excess. But an unexpected message of the card results when we include both cards that surround Temperance. Death means taking leave, completely letting go of something, and corresponds with complete renunciation and abstinence. In contrast to this, The Devil represents greed and excess. If Temperance stands between these two themes, it becomes clear that the proper proportion lies between abstinence and excess. And this is exactly what makes observing moderation so difficult. Most of us will certainly find it easier to either eat no chocolate at all (abstinence/Death) or eat an entire bar (greed/Devil) at one time; but we find taking just one single strip to be extremely abstemious. Yet, precisely here is an important message of Temperance: not abstaining from anything and yet not clinging to anything, not avoiding anything but not becoming addicted and dependent. Such an attitude in life is certainly more difficult and far more intense than sanctimoniously hovering above things, keeping out of everything from the start, not even doing many things at all, and simply being a completely well-behaved model student. On the other hand, trusting in the soul guide means getting involved in life with body and soul, but not clinging to anything!

Through its cross sum, Temperance (XIV) is connected with the Hierophant (V). If the Hierophant was the educator who prepares the hero for the journey into the outer world, Temperance can be seen as the soul guide for the journey through the night. If the Hierophant corresponds to becoming conscious of our separation from wholeness, which can also be understood as Original Sin (see page 63), it is now the soul guide who wants to lead us back to wholeness; or, put in more spiritual terms, from unholy-unwhole to holy-whole. Our term for sin has come from the Hebraic *chato* and the Greek *hamartia* and originally meant "lacking the authentic." In precisely this sense, the soul guide leads us out of our sins by letting us find our center (what is authentic). If The Hiero-phant imparted the moral code and moral qualities that led the hero to this point, then he or she can and must, from this point on, trust in a supreme force, the certainty of which only a matured conscience can give him or her on the remaining path (see figure 44).

In comparison to all the previously valid and familiar criteria, the soul guide does not differentiate between right and wrong, noble and profane, useful and useless, valuable and worthless, and also not between pleasant and unpleasant. At this point, even the valuation between good and evil taught by the high priest becomes invalid because the matured consciousness comprehends that nothing in this Creation is just good or just bad. Only the right proportion is decisive: the most extreme poison can be a healing remedy in proper dosage, while even something that is very good—lived in excess—can quickly turn into something evil.

Figure 44. The educator and guide in the outer world (Hierophant); the soul guide through the inner space and through the night (Temperance); the proper proportion (Temperance); excess (The Devil).

From here on, all that matters is the differentiation between consistency and inconsistency. And consistent in this sense is only what the person perceives, like an inner voice that gives complete certainty. C. G. Jung describes this *Vox Dei* (voice of God), as it is frequently called, to be a quiet inner voice that leads us to a "genuinely ethic reaction," a way of taking action that can completely collide with the customary ideas of morality or laws. The explosiveness that is innate here is apparent.

In any case, it requires a truly matured consciousness that cannot be conjured up through wishful thinking, and very well knows how to differentiate between self-righteousness, a know-it-all manner, a craving for recognition, or the temptations of power and a higher inspiration of its ego. For this reason, this step only occurs now, after the ego has been overcome, since this is not a *carte blanche* that allows the hero to act however he or she likes. So any person who believes that he or she has reached this point is well-advised to examine whether there really is a higher inspiration involved, or just the dubious promptings of the ego, which has perhaps just disguised itself very well. The proximity to The Devil, the following card, illustrates the great danger of confusion here.

The Bible warns of this when John says: "Do not believe all who claim to have the Spirit, but test them to find out if the spirit they have comes from God." (1st John 4:1). Lived in an immature manner, this attitude can be used to justify acts of terror and other chicanery, supposedly utopian murderous actions. But lived in a mature manner, it leads to the exemplary and imperturbably strong character of a truly devout individual who serves God and not human beings, seeking neither praise nor admiration for it.

It is always the soul guide, the *Vox Dei*, who shows the "impossible" way out of a dilemma, or a tragic debt, in which we have entangled ourselves. This is the central motif of Greek tragedy, in which the chief character becomes unavoidably guilty no matter how he or she acts. When, for example, Antigone has to decide between her duty as a sister to bury the corpse of her brother Polyneikes, and her duty to obey her uncle, the king, who has forbidden this burial, then she becomes guilty no matter what she does. The code of morality that the high priest has imparted as the foundation of the conscience fails in these cases or, particularly because of its contradictory nature, leads to the conflict. A solution results only after a great deal of suffering that involves the threat of the soul being torn apart between two opposing forces. But suddenly it is there, the irrefutable certainty that is larger and clearer than all of the convictions held before it. It not only gives us the strength to make decisions that had previously been impossible, but also helps to bear the frequently intense consequences on the remaining path in an imperturbable and straightforward manner. It is anything but certain that there will be a "happy ending" when we listen to our inner voice. Antigone ultimately had to pay for her decision with her life. However, things will go well in so far as we act with complete certainty and are willing to bear the consequences that may result from it.

But the *Vox Dei* also becomes audible in situations other than in cases of conflict. It can reach people out of the blue and can, surprisingly, give us an instruction that sometimes even leads us into such conflicts. When the Bible tells us how the voice of God commanded the prophet Hosea to marry a woman of easy virtue (Hosea 1:2) and we know what that must have meant for a pious man in those days, then we recognize how unusual and shocking such a command can be. This once again shows that Temperance has nothing to do with innocuousness. This card has nothing to do with mediocrity, or half-heartedness, and especially not with pale indecisiveness. Instead it stands for finding the combination that lets us go our very own way—which still leads to some critical walks on the razor's edge.

Keywords for TEMPERANCE

ARCHETYPE:	The soul guide
TASK:	Trusting a higher guidance, finding the right mixture
GOAL:	Unerring inner certainty, finding the center and wholeness
RISK:	Following false inspiration, mediocrity
FEELING IN LIFE:	Being carried by a great power, harmony, imperturbability, and health

THE DEVIL .

he sun has reached its position at midnight and encounters the powers of darkness here. In the same way, the hero has descended to the darkest place of his journey. Here in the labyrinth of the underworld, the lost treasure, the beautiful prisoner, the herb of life—or whatever the value that is hard to find may be—is guarded by a terrible monster, a dangerous dragon, or a sinister adversary.

With these images, myths and fairy tales describe the menacing thing that surfaces from the unconscious. We feel it as soon as we come into contact with its powers, since it is something very different from calmly contemplating the unconscious. In this true contact, we can easily be overcome by fear and panicky terror, which C. G. Jung has explained through the analogy that this encounter has with mental disorder:

The Devil
In the Realm of the Shadow

> The intellect has no objection to "analysing" the unconscious as a passive object; on the contrary such an activity would coincide with our rational expectations. But to let the unconscious go its own way and to experience it as a reality is something beyond the courage and capacity of the average European. He prefers simply not to understand this problem. For the spiritually weak-kneed this is the better course, since the thing is not without its dangers.[1]

However, at this point of the journey, we are concerned with encountering and experiencing this dark side of our being.

Since in the Christian West the Devil has been declared as the *summum malum*, the sum of all evil, all the shadow aspects are united within him. This makes the meaning of this card extremely complex, and the tasks at this archetypal stage cannot be reduced to a single motif.

This certainly deals with something unheard-of in the double sense of the word—precisely everything that we have never heard about in our life, and everything that we reject as outrageous in the

---

[1] C. G. Jung, "Individual Dream Symbolism in Relation to Alchemy," in *Psychology and Alchemy*, CW, vol. 12, ¶ 60.

Dread at the sight of the inner demons
[detail] (Sistine Chapel, Vatican).

unshakable conviction that it certainly has nothing to do with us. These are actions, motives, wishes, intentions, thoughts, qualities that are deeply embarrassing to us, that fill us with dread, that we are ashamed of, that we have only perceived in others up to now. However, we have perceived them there repeatedly, urgently, and with indignation.

Modes of behavior, attitudes, and comments that can get us terribly upset, that can make us deeply indignant, are, in all seriousness, something we must recognize as belonging to us—even though we found them to be more fitting in others. Here in the sinister realm of the shadow lives everything that we have suppressed so well, that we know hardly anything about, or that we know nothing at all about. This is everything that we dreaded before when we perceived it—everything that we would be ashamed of down to the bones if someone would "catch" us at it—if we would even catch ourselves. And now we should and must recognize and accept all of this as belonging to us. No wonder we only do this with great fear, reluctance, and uneasiness.

We have Albert Camus to thank for a highly impressive description of such a relentless self-confession, a truly merciless self-revelation that even animates us to imitate it. In his book *The Fall*,[2] he tells the story of a respected, cultivated, and successful attorney from the best circles, who has a completely impeccable image of himself. Yet, one night on a deserted bridge he hears laughter behind him. This laughter returns time and again and refuses to let go of him until he inexorably admits who he really is; until he sees through the vanity of his ego, perceives his enormous shadow, and comprehends the true motives behind his refined character and all his noble deeds.

At this dark place, everything that wants to be alive within us, but

---

2 Cf. Albert Camus, *The Fall* (New York: Random House, 1991), p. 34ff.

As soon as the alert intellect that controls everything
wants to sleep, the suppressed demons torment it
("The Sleep of Reason Gives Birth to Monsters,"
Francisco de Goya, Morat Institute, Vienna).

is not permitted to be, barely manages to stay
alive in a miserable shadow existence. These are
the unpopular "inner people," those whom our
ego considers to be unacceptable in good society
and therefore flatly disowns. They find themselves in an *oubliette*, that truly hellish dungeon
that is too low for a person to stand up and too
short to stretch out. This is where an evil-doer
was thrown in the Middle Ages in order to simply be forgotten there. Our ego deals with the
unloved sides of our personality in a no less

Lucifer watches over the split-off parts of the souls that have fallen to him (woodcut by Gustave Doré).

157

The wrangling in Hell corresponds to the sticky, undifferentiated, chaotic condition of the neglected function of consciousness [detail] (Luca Signorelli, Dom of Orvieto).

brutal manner. They are mercilessly locked away and forgotten. No wonder they become demons that plague our consciousness—and not just our nightmares.

In the language of the fairy tale, this is the place of the souls that have been sold. Here in the underworld, Lucifer watches over the parts of our being that have been split off, over everything that we human beings do not consider as belonging to us. And this is precisely where lies what we are lacking to be whole, which is at the same time the source of our mistakes.

Seen in psychological terms, the treasure hard to find is difficult to attain in relation to the aspect of the four functions of consciousness that we have not developed, that has remained unconscious, and that is lacking in our conscious mind (see page 89ff.). We are vehemently confronted with its lack and the resulting mistakes at this point. This occurs either because we unavoidably meet this characteristic time and time again in the world around us, and have no choice but to confront it, or because we finally comprehend that we must turn to this aspect because we are lacking in it for our wholeness.

Above all, the unpleasant thing is that this side of our being has remained underdeveloped, coarse, and primitive. While we have developed the other functions of consciousness with elegance and refined them over a period of many years, this neglected part has lagged behind more and more, remaining uncivilized, inferior, sticky, and chaotic. This is why we dislike it, find it annoying, actually think it is superfluous and unnecessary, and despise it—at least in secret—when we experience it in other people. If we now must learn to develop this function of consciousness ourselves, then this is not only an unaccustomed and troublesome task; above all, it is time-consuming. It appears to us that we must put on dirty glasses, even though all of our other three pairs are so clear and clean. It is as if we must show ourselves in public with a seedy lowlife or a down-at-the-heel whore. And this is why we have so stubbornly refused to even start at all up to now.

Our consciousness is frequently arrogant enough to believe that everything we have suppressed or forgotten is no longer there. These suppressed and forgotten things have only become unconscious, yet they still remain effective. We are simply no longer conscious of them. And this contains a great danger for us since we can only control, in a responsible manner, the things of which we are conscious. A sailor who knows the ways of the wind can even sail against the wind with its help. But if he were to be unaware of this force, he would become its plaything. The same applies for our unlived shad-

What we are lacking causes us to backslide time and again (Anne-Louis Girodet Trioson, Louvre, Paris).

ow aspects. To know nothing of them does not mean that they do not exist or are even ineffective.

Each of us knows moments in which "the devil made me do it." We use this phrase to describe a situation in which a force suddenly arises that lies with the Devil because we have completely split it off and suppressed it from ourselves. But suddenly, this demonized side will inundate our entire consciousness—we could even say it occupies it—and lets us do things for which we have no explanations. In the face of this, we are stunned as we ask ourselves how this could happen to us. Psychology calls these non-integrated portions of our personality "autonomous complexes," which lead something like a vagabond existence in our soul. They move, so to speak, like shady characters outside the organizing power of our consciousness and wait only for an advantageous, unguarded moment—such as in a very excited or even drunken state—to occupy the consciousness so that they can live out their impulses without any inhibitions. They let us do things that we subsequently experience as foreign to our ego since our ego does not know—and does not want to know—these sides of ourselves.

But even when things do not go so far that the Devil gets hold of us, when our consciousness actually believes it is in control, our unlived shadow aspects constantly hard-press and influence us. Who of us is not susceptible to seduction or manipulation? And don't we all do things that we actually wanted to stop doing long ago? Probably all human beings fight this battle against their own weaknesses, the inner seducer. And those who believe that they have overcome this problem are possibly wise, but probably just naive. Because these shadow aspects are lacking in our wholeness and because we do not want to admit them to ourselves, they become our mistakes and weaknesses, the roots of our bondage. What we are lacking makes us possessed, and drags us down over and over, perhaps just to draw attention to itself, so that we do not forget it. These unloved and unlived aspects want to be released from their dungeon; they want to take form and be lived. This is why, despite our good intentions, they let us relapse to make sure we cannot ever believe we can manage without them.

Even if we have imagined it in a completely different way, we are at the place of healing here. As long as we think that this shadow realm does not belong to us, we remain one-sided and unwhole. But these considerations should not be misunderstood as a challenge to simply and unrestrainedly work off all previously unlived aggressions with a neighbor, at work, or at home. Nor does it mean just existing according to the pleasure principle from now on and uninhibitedly "acting like a pig." Above all, this is a matter of admitting the suppressed tendencies and desires in the first place, and then looking for a possibility of integrating them into the conscious personality, and living them out in a responsible manner. Then it is possible for what was destructive to once again become constructive because it has returned to its own place.[3] This is not meant in an innocuous way. People who become aware of the shadow and live the previously suppressed aspects are never harmless. They can be highly troublesome, provocative, or even shocking. But they know what they are doing and do it consciously and thus can assume the responsibility.

Whatever should not or cannot be does not let go of us until we—in the double sense of the word—let it be. But the more we fight and suppress it, the more we will be occupied with it, and the more it will attract and fascinate us. As long as we are not willing or capable of seeing the power within us that we consider to be dark, we must of necessity perceive it in others, which is naturally also much more pleasant for the ego. However, our own shadow will consequently threaten us from the outside to a growing degree. This results in personal animosities, monstrous suspicions, and the indefensible assigning of blame, as well as all the personal or collective conspiracy theories, according to which the world is infiltrated by a group that wants to seize all the power for itself. According to fashion trends and political position, examples of these are (or were) the Communists, Freemasons, Zionists, drug lords, fundamentalists, witches, Jews, Greens, neo-Nazis, heretics, Scientologists, Bolshevists, Mafioso, Jesuits, major capitalists, or the CIA. The perfidious thing about this is that the accused groups are not allowed the slightest opportunity to shake off this collective projection. Wherever something is projected, people are completely stubborn because the otherwise wakeful intellect would then become immune to even the most convincing arguments. There is no chance for the scapegoat. Whatever it does will be construed against it, intensifying all the previous suspicions.

Fighting the shadow in the outside world always corresponds with an inner pull. Whatever is suppressed exercises such a strong fascination on its part that, more frequently than anyone else, we get involved with precisely these terrible people or situations that we fight so sincerely. But, even worse, is that what is suppressed within us either secretly has us do exactly what should not be done—especially since a self-satisfied ego will very quickly grant a special license to

---

[3] Cf. Marie-Louise von Franz, *Shadow and Evil in Fairy-Tales* (Zurich: Spring, 1974), p. 43.

itself—or has us do something in all openness that appears to be good and noble. Yet when we take a closer look at it, this is not even slightly better. When, for example, a priest wants to drive out all the devils, in his holy overzealousness he may create an exorcistic orgy that has the distinct characteristics of a black mass. When a simple-minded citizen feels compelled to be a pornography-hunter and—to his great regret—must look at all the dirt that he fights, he therefore consumes much more of it than any average person. In the process, his ego is well out of it because it is permitted to do the dirtiest things and still keep his reputation spotless. When animal activists kill people to protect the animals, when people fight for peace with weapons, when the "squeaky-cleans" of the nation are suddenly found to be less than innocent themselves, when people who believe in a loving God bestially torture and murder others in religious zealotry, when the great liberators of the people become tyrants and despots, when gurus suck their followers dry—then people have become enslaved by their shadows in an overzealousness that is more hasty than holy. And they usually fail to notice it.

But here, in the depth of the night, dwells a very special shadow that we encounter time and again in the course of our lives. It is our unconscious opposite sexuality, which Jung called the anima or animus. Both always have, like all inner images, two sides: a light and a dark one. Long ago, we already encountered the light side (or polarity) of the anima or animus—back when we fell head over heels in love for the first time. At this moment, the woman encounters her animus and a man lets himself be enchanted by his anima. Such a magical power can only come from the unconscious, since nothing else can enchant our conscious mind.

When we become infatuated we have fallen in love with our inner image. The person who causes our heart to beat faster will have the matching hook for us to hang our picture on. Something within him or her makes this projection possible. But this certain something is quite small in comparison to what we experience; perhaps it corresponds to the relationship between the picture and the hook. Experience has shown that the infatuation phase rarely lasts longer than six months. Then the wonderful picture gets more and more cracks in it, becomes brittle, and allows increasingly more strange, unpleasant contours to emerge. Although we still do our best to save the original picture, sooner or later we will angrily accuse the fairy-tale prince or the woman of our dreams: "You sure have changed!" and naturally mean "for the worst!" We insult the other person with "false packaging," feel deceived and disillusioned, and believe that we final-

Medusa with the snake-wreathed head (Michelangelo Merisi de Caravaggio, Uffizi, Florence).

ly recognize his or her true nature. However, our partner has not changed at all—only our power of projection has weakened more and more each day. For some people, this is a reason to throw everything away and quickly look for a new projection surface in order to yield to the intoxication of falling in love once again for another six months. Others are willing, with time, to become more mature and gradually learn to differentiate the image of the soul from reality. For them, the actual relationship only begins when the infatuation has passed.[4]

❦ With The Devil, we have now landed at the dark counterpole of the anima and animus. If the bright aspects of our soul image enchanted us until life taught us to recognize our own projections within it, we now feel ourselves deeply threatened by the dark aspect of our inner image. But this time it is even more difficult to understand that these are our own images, and not the people to whom we transfer these shadow aspects. This is why we really do everything in order to prove the contrary. We are completely certain that these are not projections, but very real dangers that threaten us. We think they must therefore be banned and destroyed as quickly as possible. But as much as we may threaten our shadow, strike out at it, burn it, or try to get rid of it in some other way, oddly enough it always immediately appears again. It belongs to us, and we can shake it off as little as we can our physical shadow.

The patriarchally toned world of classical antiquity has almost exclusively handed down feminine shadow images. Above all, this

---

[4] For more details, see Hajo Banzhaf and Brigitte Theler, *Secrets of Love and Partnership* (York Beach, ME: Samuel Weiser, 1998).

includes the dark side of Medusa, who has her equivalent in the sinister aspect of the Indian goddess Kali and continued on in the demonization of the woman and obsessive belief in witches during the Middle Ages.

When a man blindly transfers the dark pole of his anima to his partner and is absolutely certain that this is exactly how she is, it will certainly be difficult for her to have a harmonious relationship with him. The same applies to a woman who transfers the inner berserker, the torturer, or the wicked fiend without restraint onto her partner. As difficult as it may have been to see through the light projection and accept it as one's own, it is much more arduous to understand that these dark projections are our own images as well, even if we perceive and experience them so closely and convincingly in our partner. The more stubbornly we close our eyes to this insight, the more frequently and intensely these shadows will appear in our life. We feel deeply disappointed by all the people in whom we are suddenly "forced" to perceive these negative characteristics. With a holy rage, we even separate from those who are closest to us. We leave those people we had once loved, and swear that we will be more careful the next time. But as much as we attempt to be careful and examine and probe other people, as soon as the next infatuation dies down, we are horrified to discover that we have once again gotten involved with a devil—or a witch. Then, at some point, we believe that we have collected enough bad experience so that we can now talk about men or women in general with authority. And our opinion of them is naturally devastating! In proud resignation, we lean back and decide never to get involved in a relationship again. Never again!

Perhaps it dawns on us now that we carry these annoying and disappointing experiences within ourselves and trigger them over and over in our interactions with others. It is our shadow that falls on our surrounding world, and we must recognize and integrate this inner shadow world within ourselves instead of fighting it with fire and sword in the outside world. In any case, it is the message of many myths that it is not the loner who reaches the goal, but only the hero who lets himself or herself be led by the soul guide of the opposite sex. This concept

The Indian mother goddess Kali.

should give us food for thought. Only when we have intensively confronted the other sex can we become whole. Embittered retreat, harsh hardening, or faked (to oneself) independence are not solutions. Those who fail in relationships, or who avoid the opposite sex for long periods of time, fail in an essential part of their lives. A single will always just be half of one whole.

The tarot card shows us Adam and Eve bound in chains to the power of The Devil. The card represents dependence, addiction, and bondage, implying that we are doing something against our own convictions, against our will. The reason for this is apparent: we are not free, but bound, and can therefore be manipulated. However, as we can see on the card, the chains are loose enough so that the two could free themselves from them. But to do so, they must understand what keeps them imprisoned. And precisely here is the problem. It is tremendously difficult for us to recognize the causes of our dependencies and addictions.

Behind every addiction there is a search that has failed. The correlations are often so suppressed that we no longer know what we are actually looking for. Often, we do not even know that we are searching for anything at all. We only feel the consequences, such as continuing to smoke even though we have given it up so many times. At least on the first half of the path, we usually attempt to solve such problems with the "masculine" method of getting rid of them, true to the motto of: "If I want to, then I can!" or "It would be a joke if I couldn't get this under control!" Some apparently succeed at this. With great toughness, they suppress the symptom and believe that they have solved the entire problem as a result. But this is not the solution. No smoker turns into a non-smoker in this way. At best he or she becomes a non-smoking smoker. Sooner or later, the problem will create another symptom in order not to be forgotten, and the consciousness only recognizes the correlation involved in rare cases. But many people backslide before they get this far, and fail because of their good intentions, with which we all know the path to Hell is paved. And this is exactly where we find ourselves at this point.

The actual problem lies here in the shadow world. When we solve it, the symptom is also cured. It is difficult to pick up the track of the actual problem—to find out what we are *really* looking for—those unlived aspects within us that want to come to life. Brooding and reflecting on this is the least effective approach, for our consciousness will continue to make suggestions that bypass what's actually wrong because these aspects have split off for a "good reason." The ego feels itself very much threatened by what we lack and has banned it to the shadow world. The ego would prefer to "be damned" rather than to permit this part of ourselves access to consciousness. Yet, the self, which wants to lead us to wholeness, is concerned with having us encounter the theme for which we are searching; this applies even if our consciousness absolutely does not want to recognize this, and stubbornly denies that these aspects could have anything at all to do with us. If we truly want to comprehend, we will be helped by mindfully observing anything that we encounter over and over, or that with which we are frequently inwardly preoccupied, or that which shows itself to us in dreams.

If our intellect does not resist insights, but lets us comprehend that running away is no solution, that particularly where we want to "get the hell out," where we get all worked up and indignant, is precisely the place where the buried treasure may be, then we have achieved a great deal. And oddly enough, the solution to this problem is not even necessary to understand it. The right thing happening suffices. This means that our addiction is resolved at the moment we take the right step, even if we never perceive or even understand what is going on and how these two themes are related.

It is also conspicuous how—especially in supposedly esoteric or new age circles—that people tend to steer clear of anything that looks like the devil, black, the occult, or darkness. Some people do not seem to see any contradiction in constantly speaking of healing and wholeness and, at the same moment, claiming to not have anything to do with the "darkness" or even immediately changing it into white wherever it is encountered. White is therefore often the preferred clothing and constant light meditation the desperate attempt to keep everything dark and evil away. The psychological consequence can be a persecution complex. As we know, the unconscious always behaves in a compensatory manner to the conscious mind, so a morbidly white consciousness will necessarily conjure up a jet-black unconscious. And since the ego cannot be had by these dark contents, they must of necessity constellate on the outside as the evil from which a person feels increasingly threatened. C. G. Jung expressed his concerns as follows: "One does not become enlightened by imagining figures of light, but by making the darkness conscious. The latter procedure, however, is disagreeable and therefore not popular."[5]

---

[5] C. G. Jung, "The Philosophical Tree," in *Alchemical Studies*, CW, vol. 13, ¶ 335.

It must seem rather odd that the Devil is called Lucifer, which means "Bringer of Light." How can the force that we see as the quintessence of darkness and evil be a bringer of light? Our ego is extremely clever at always placing us in the right light so that we actually look very good in comparison to others. Not that our self-assessment is completely wrong, but it is extremely one-sided, because it completely disregards essential aspects. And therefore, we know very little of ourselves as long as we just listen to the flattery of our ego. However, if we then encounter our shadow side and recognize that it also belongs to us, we will actually see the light, that this is what we *also* are. This is why the Gnostics like to compare evil with a broken mirror that has fallen from Heaven. A mirror has no picture of its own. It shows anyone who looks in it a picture that he or she could never have seen without this mirror. The lucid aspect of the Devil lies in this consciousness-expanding insight.

As long as we know nothing of our shadow, we think we are harmless. "The man who recognizes his shadow," says Jung, "knows very well that he is not harmless."[6] The less we recognize the darkness within ourselves, the less we think the other person is capable of it. If we play ourselves down, we also play down the people with whom we interact at the same time. We also avoid necessary confrontations by simply assuming that all people are good. Our ego flatters us with the idea that we are so full of love for all people that, if only because of this, we find ourselves on a higher level of development than all the poor unilluminated individuals who still must come to terms with life and unpleasant people in such a hard and conflict-filled manner. Yet, it is probably less overdeveloped humanitarianism than pure cowardice that prevents us from becoming committed to what we believe in, or fighting for our rights. This may frequently make us victims because we don't want to see how others take advantage of our harmlessness, cheat us, or make fun of us.

Just as we shy away from encountering our own shadow, we also avoid confrontations with the shadow aspects of others. We prefer to gloss over and play down what we don't want to see. The apparent advantage is a world that remains intact. We also avoid many conflicts. But the obvious disadvantage is not only that the person becomes a victim over and over, but that we cling to the role and the consciousness level of an innocent child who cannot believe how terrible the world is. Perhaps we learned as a child that it suffices to just be well-

---

[6] C. G. Jung, "Psychology of the Transference," in *The Practice of Psychotherapy*, CW, vol. 16, ¶ 452.

Figure 45. The path of the free decision of the heart (The Lovers) and its opposite, the imprisonment in dependency and passionate entanglement (The Devil).

behaved. But this childlike attitude soon conveys a ridiculous impression in adults and becomes increasingly problematic. Marie-Louise von Franz says:

> The only way, therefore, not to walk through the world like an innocent well-brought-up fool, protected by father and mother from the evils of this world and therefore cheated and lied to and stolen from at every corner, is to go down into the depths of one's own evil, which enables one usually to develop the instinctual recognition of corresponding elements in other people.[7]

The cards The Lovers (VI) and The Devil (XV) are associated with each other (see figure 45). In the Waite Tarot, this correlation is highlighted even further with a similar motif. We see Adam and Eve before and after the Fall. On The Lovers, they are under the protection of Raphael, the guardian of the Tree of Life, the healer of Earth and human beings. This archangel is also considered the guide through the underworld and the vanquisher of the dark angel Asael, the Old Testament equivalent of the Devil, who has the power over the people on the 15th card. The connection of these two cards challenges us to separate from entanglements, dependencies, and bondage (The Devil) and take the path of the free decision of the heart (The Lovers).

---

[7] Marie-Louise von Franz, *Individuation in Fairy Tales* (Boston: Shambhala, 1990), p. 10.

Both cards also prove to be the opposites of the same experience. This is an insight that actually conceals something monstrous within itself. There is no other place where we experience ourselves so noble, so good and pure, and believe we are completely without evil than when we love from the depths of our hearts. But the link between these two cards shows that even there, where we are absolutely convinced of our pure motives and our true love, the dark polarity in the form of greed, lustfulness, a hunger for power, possessiveness, and other heinous aspects exists. The reverse is also true: even where we only see evil in the other person, where we swear revenge and would most like to destroy that person, there is always a light polarity, even if it is suppressed. Behind anger, hate, and loathing are concealed feelings of love that have been condensed to the point of intolerability.

The perception that these two polarities actually belong together and, just like light and dark—like day and night—can only form a whole when they are together, is extremely intolerable for us, especially in our most noble and holy feelings. We would love to keep only the light side for ourselves and send the dark side to Hell. The most heartrending aspect of this tension is expressed in Faust's famous words to Wagner, the representative of naive harmlessness: "Only one aspiration thou hast known, Oh never seek to know the other, never! Two souls, alas! Within my bosom throne; One from the other wildly longs to sever."[8]

---

[8] Johann Wolfgang von Goethe, *Faust I*, line 1110.

Keywords for THE DEVIL

ARCHETYPE:	The adversary
TASK:	Overcoming inner resistance, insight into unlived shadow aspects, making dark things conscious, taking back projections
GOAL:	Understanding one's own errors, discovering unknown sides of one's own being, freeing oneself from addictions.
RISK:	Becoming enslaved to the shadow, backsliding, immoderation, lustfulness, power struggles
FEELING IN LIFE:	Bondage, dependence, possession, being in the grips of the Devil

After the hero has succeeded in forcefully entering the underworld, the important thing is to now liberate the lost treasure, the soul that has been sold, or whatever is held prisoner here from the power of the adversary. This task corresponds to The Tower. It represents victory over the guard, killing the dragon, the sudden bursting open of the prison, freeing the captive soul, and pushing open the gates of the underworld.

The card shows a flash of lightning hitting The Tower and knocking off its crown. Such a crown, which is closed on top, means not recognizing any higher power above oneself. This allows The Tower to become a symbol for haughtiness, megalomania, and even ego-glorification, like the famous Tower of Babel.

The Tower
Dramatic Liberation

As a warning finger of God, the lightning symbolizes an outer event that leads to the radical change or collapse of an old order. It can just as easily be a flash of inspiration that suddenly makes clear how wrong our previous ideas were, and how much we have built upon sand. But the meaning of the card can be best illustrated by comparing it to the IV of Wands, which forms the opposite to The Tower within the minor arcana (see figure 46 on page 174).

Both motifs show a large structure: a fortress and a tower. The same people in similar clothing can be seen on both cards. While they joyfully leave the fortress on the IV of Wands, they are being thrown out on the card The Tower. In order to understand the correlation between the two cards, we can imagine an ideal home for the time of our childhood in the motif of the IV of Wands. The fortress in the background stands—like the parental home—for the sense of security that we feel behind us while we openly and curiously go out to explore the world, accompanied by the deep certainty that we can always return to the safety of the parental home. So the IV of Wands means peace, openness, and a sense of security within a harmonious framework. However, when we still live in the same child's room and Mother continues to make the bed and breakfast for us when we are 40 years old, then the condition that originally was harmonious and correct has become too narrow, if only for the reason that we have grown. This

Figure 46. The Tower and the IV of Wands as polar opposites.

much too narrow structure must therefore be shattered. As a result, The Tower means that something we have long held onto, which was once completely appropriate, has now become too limited, too naive, outdated, or encrusted, and is ultimately only a prison for us.

So this card can mean the collapse of a restricted view of the world, a value system that is outdated or too naive, liberation from constricting conditioning, as well as the breakdown of a false self-image. At the same time, The Tower can also represent a breakthrough to greater freedom. The problem is that we have actually become quite accustomed to our prison. It was too confined, but, on the other hand, we were well-acquainted with it. And we do cling to what we know, even if this is just the old familiar misery. This is why at first we usually experience the upheaval that The Tower symbolizes with fear and often as a catastrophe. Only in retrospect do we recognize the decisive liberation that it included.

Whether caused by the outside world or from within, the lightning striking always means a sudden change that lets our foregone conclusions collapse. This may be a notice of termination, a sudden separation, the failure of fixed expectations, or a shock to our self-image. In all of these cases, we become aware that reality is larger and different than we had imagined it to be. And this is precisely the significant insight waiting for us at this point.

In its endeavor to eliminate any insecurity, to "explain away" the uncertainties, and to gain control of the unpredictable, our ego has created its concept of reality. In the process, it has drawn the boundaries within which it feels secure. Egos with the same ideas like to join groups of common interests, which have the advantage of mutually validating and approving of each other. This, in turn, is good for each individual ego, and increases its trust in the mutual world of ideas, the only "true" reality. Egos with other ideas are shut out and, at best, laughed at or derided because they are "so dumb," "unenlightened," "don't understand," or "simply have no idea." But if the concepts of others are experienced as too threatening, the ego believes it must fight them and

The Tower of Babel, symbol of megalomania (Pieter Bruegel, Kunsthistorisches Museum, Vienna).

even destroy them, if necessary. So the ego likes to go through life with the firm conviction of knowing and having explored reality very well; yet it is concerned with nothing else but confirming its own concepts, once they have been established, at all times and in all places.

We love the pictures that we make of reality much more than reality itself. We don't even notice that our ideas have pushed themselves between us and reality, that they actually separate us from the immediate experience of reality. Like a foregone conclusion, we consider the images that our thoughts create—fed by memories, wishes, fear, or greed—to be true. Our intellect is much less interested in perceiving the objective reality than in clinging to an advantageous, comfortable, but above all familiar concept. For example, a man may secretly have had a suspicion that something was wrong with his partnership. But he had always quickly pushed the thought aside and persuaded himself that everything was actually wonderful; otherwise, he would ultimately have a problem and would have to question himself, perhaps even make changes in his life. It is naturally much more comfortable to deny

We often make ourselves comfortable in our Ivory Tower, but reality hits hard when the Ivory Tower collapses, as it inevitably does ("The Fall of the Giants," Guilio Romano, Sala dei Giganti, Palazzo del Te, Mantua).

all the circumstantial evidence and persuade oneself that everything is fine, or at least normal, since, after all, neighbors and friends are not doing any better. But then comes the day when he is stunned to perceive the reality behind his images. And this is when the lovely palace, or the Ivory Tower, in which his ego has made itself so comfortably at home, collapses. To his horror, he discovers that reality is completely different than he had always imagined. This is The Tower.

The concepts we cling to do not even have to be ones that make us happy. We can just as well suffer from the images that we have made of reality. The Greek philosopher Epictetus discovered 2000 years ago that things are not what disconcert us, but the opinions we have of things. They can become the obsessions we use to make our lives sour. When the ego, for example, gets set upon the fixed idea that elevators are dangerous, then the respective person will tremble during every ride in an elevator, firmly convinced that it will at least get stuck, if not crash. Sooner or later, the person will begin to avoid all elevators, and will attribute more truth to his fears than the most reasonable argument and the value of experience. The price for such obsessions is, in addition to an increasing limitation in the freedom of movement, more suffering in life. In these cases, The Tower can indicate a key experience or a flash of inspiration that makes the breakthrough to freedom possible for us.

The walls of The Tower prevent us from seeing the greater whole. Since they, like all boundaries, separate us from the unity of all things, they must collapse. This thought is in Krishnamurti's words about "emptying" consciousness, its de-conditioning and purification from the past.[1] However, our ego very much clings to its narrow-minded concepts, like a dog with a bone, and an intensive and surprising experience is often required for a breakthrough to occur. This is why fairy tales are so tremendously radical when it comes to destroying evil; they always consider evil to be whatever wants to prevent consciousness. This is why evil is so mercilessly eliminated in fairy tales.

On a deeper level, The Tower opens the door to an immense truth by letting an old, conditioned value system collapse. It shakes the divine order that the Western mind so loves—like non-ambiguity, clarity, and logic—to its foundations. This is precisely the basic precondition for the experience of higher truth, the unity of all things, which must appear paradoxical in its being. Breaking through the constriction of our blocks in consciousness has always been the goal of great teachers of wisdom who—such as the legendary Sufi master Mullah Nasrdin—always shake up fixed concepts through unexpected jumps from one idea to the other. In the same way, they like to raise questions that lead familiar foregone conclusions to the point of absurdity, to our surprise. For the same reason, those who practice Zen Buddhism are given paradox riddles (koans), that logic cannot solve, for their meditation. The consciousness struggling for clarity has a problem with this.

Despite all of this, we should not underestimate what it means when the tower of constricted or false consciousness is burst. "A collapse of the conscious attitude is no small matter," as C. G. Jung emphasizes. "It always feels like the end of the world, as though everything had tumbled back into original chaos. One feels delivered up, disoriented, like a rudderless ship that is abandoned to the moods of the elements. So at least it seems. In reality, however, one has fallen back upon the collective unconscious, which now takes over the leadership."[2] But he also warns that there are just as many cases in which the collapse meant a catastrophe that destroyed life as such, where an

---

[1] Cf. Gunturu Vanamali, *The Play of God: Visions of the Life of Krishnamurti* (San Diego: Blue Dove, 1996).
[2] C. G. Jung, "Negative Attempts to Free the Individuality from the Collective Psyche," in *Two Essays on Analytical Psychology*, CW, vol. 7 ¶ 254.

inner voice gives life a new direction. The Tower that we experience quite naturally depends upon how we approach it, and how much we have matured on the path already taken. The more spongelike, condescending, or pompous we are, the more dramatic this experience will be. Jung even said: "An inflated consciousness is . . . hypnotized by itself and can therefore not be argued with. It inevitably dooms itself to calamities that must strike it dead."[3]

Translated to the developmental path of a human being, there are a number of equivalents for The Tower experience. For one thing, this concerns the liberation of the soul that has been sold, the raising of the treasure that is hard to find. It is a symbol of the fourth, previously neglected and scorned function of consciousness (see page 89) and the related upheavals, shocks, and re-evaluations in our view of the world. On the other hand, this involves living something that we had never risked living because we did not have the courage, because we had sold our soul for security, harmlessness, or another false currency. As a result, The Tower can mean that we "drop a bombshell," break out of circumstances that are much too constricted for us, quit a job, simply no longer play along, or suddenly show ourselves from a side that no one (including ourselves) ever knew was there.

In the same way, The Tower can represent overcoming pettiness, for bursting the chains that bound and restricted our hearts up to now. In the fairy tale of the Frog King, there were three cracks around his chest when the iron bonds burst from the heart of Faithful Heinrich, whereby it was said each time:

"Heinrich, the carriage is falling apart."
"No, master, it's only an iron ring.
I had it forged around my heart
For fear that it would break in two…"

But this concerns overcoming what has influenced our eyes up to now, what exercised unconscious power over us and let us do things for which we had no explanation, which crippled us in many respects, and kept us from living. Seen in this way, The Tower corresponds with the central motif of many myths and fairy tales that tell us of overcoming the adversary, or the dragon, who always frightens and terrifies the entire world. This is followed by the liberation of what it holds captive. In one sense, this monster can be understood as the inner

[3] C. G. Jung, "Epilogue," in *Psychology and Alchemy*, CW, vol. 12, ¶ 563.

resistance that rigorously lets us say in the face of our task in life: "Anything, but not that!" Or, even more drastically: "I'd rather die!" (see page 132). Without a doubt, overcoming this resistance and doing what has been completely out of the question up to now is an intensive Tower experience.

On the other hand, we can also understand the dragon as an inner controlling authority, a powerful father or mother image from which we have not yet been able to free ourselves. We have been at its mercy, and it will continue to keep us from going our own way until we can overcome it. This is the theme of many myths and fairy tales. For example, Hansel being pitiably imprisoned in the gingerbread house—an enticing paradise of desire—in the deep woods, and the witch wanting to devour him, corresponds with a completely unconscious (= dark woods) dark mother image to which he is helplessly enslaved until Gretel, his anima, saves him. We have the reverse case in Sleeping Beauty, but the animus takes 100 years before he frees her from the power field of the dark fairy. Such fairy tales as Rumpelstiltskin, in which a poor miller awakens the highest expectations of his daughter by telling the king that she can spin gold, tells of overcoming the father image and the related expectations.

Without wanting to reduce the messages of these fairy tales to one interpretation, they show us how important it is to step out of the shadow of an overpowering father or mother image in order to be free, as well as capable of having a relationship. No matter whether we have become enslaved to a positive or negative parental image, as long as it has power over us we are not free to openly encounter the opposite sex. Either we are so entangled in a love-hate relationship with the respective parent that we never get around to opening up to another person, or we are so dominated by the dark aspect that we are terrified and keep clear of the opposite sex. Even if this inner image has a positive nature, we must still free ourselves of it. Otherwise, we will constantly compare people in the outside world to this inner image. And since soul images are complete, which we unfortunately cannot say about the men and women "out there," they cause disappointment and the failure of one relationship after the other. The loyalty to the inner image will remain unbroken.

Moreover, the moment in which Perseus cuts off Medusa's head can be understood on one level as overcoming an exceedingly powerful inner mother image. He only succeeded in this heroic deed with the help of his anima, in the form of the protecting goddess Athene, with whom he was in constant contact. She gave him his shoes, sickle, bag, and shield. She led him to the Gorgons and gave him a step-by-step

explanation of what he had to do. Without her support, he would certainly have failed. But with the help of the feminine, he was capable of overcoming an excessively powerful feminine image.

Oedipus, on the other hand, attempted this by using the power of his intellect, without the help of his anima. As a result, he achieved only an apparent victory. He solved the riddle presented to him by the Sphinx, and freed the city of Thebes from her terror. But he was not interested in the riddle that the Sphinx herself embodied, as a symbol of the unfathomable feminine, nor did he perceive or solve it. In victorious arrogance, he mistakenly considered the part to be whole and let himself be crowned king as the great overcomer. His anima, his soul guide, would certainly have given him better advice. Instead, he unconsciously married his mother and put himself completely at the mercy of the feminine, the inner mother image, which he believed he had overcome. When his false worldview—his tower—collapsed and he was forced to perceive the reality behind the concept that had

Perseus overcomes Medusa. His protecting goddess Athene is at the right of the picture (vase, British Museum, London).

Oedipus only achieved an apparent victory over the Sphinx. He had attempted to overcome the monster with the power of his intellect, but without the help of his anima (drinking bowl, Vatican Museum, Rome).

The barque crosses the underworld. Ra, the Sun God, is threatened by Apophis. Seth stands at the tip of the barque (Papyrus Cherit-Webeshet, Egyptian Museum, Cairo).

been a foregone conclusion for him, it was too much for him and he became insane.

The myth of the Egyptian Sun God Ra's nighttime sea journey also tells of a complete upheaval of familiar concepts at the midnight hour. Here, at the deepest point of his journey, Ra encounters the greatest of all dangers. Apophis, the snake of the nighttime sea, sucks dry the underground Nile with one single gulp so that the barque gets stuck on a sandbank. The Sun God cannot continue his journey and there would not be a new morning if not for Seth. Seth conquers Apophis and forces the snake to spit out the water so that the barque can continue its journey. Although this may sound like a harmless story to us, it must have sounded virtually unbelievable to the ears of the ancient Egyptians. Seth was considered the arch villain and greatest enemy of the Sun God during the day. But here, at the midnight

Figure 47. The Tower in the Tarot of Marseille.
The crown is knocked off by a feather.

Figure 48. The Chariot shows the departure into the outer world while The Tower symbolizes
the breakthrough on the journey through the night.

hour, he is the only one who can make sure that the barque continues to move. This was so outrageous that people dared not say his name and just whispered: "The greatest sorcerer of all times helps the great Ra here." But everyone knew who this great sorcerer was. The impressive message of this ancient tradition is: in this darkest hour, the black-and-white valuations of daytime consciousness collapses. They no longer apply here. Even the one who we have experienced as our greatest enemy can be the only one who is capable of helping us achieve the decisive breakthrough here. This background also allows the Biblical commandment of "love your enemies" to appear in a new light.

In the old tarot cards, the crown of The Tower is knocked off by a feather (see figure 47). As the sign of Maat (page 130), it is the symbol of divine justice that destroys what is wrong and imbalanced.

The Tower (XVI) is associated with the card The Chariot (VII) through its cross sum (figure 48). If The Chariot shows the departure of the hero into the outer world, then The Tower stands for the decisive breakthrough on the journey through the night.

Keywords for THE TOWER

ARCHETYPE:	The liberation
TASK:	Bursting boundaries that are too narrow, breaking out of outdated, encrusted structures, overcoming black-and-white thinking, "dropping a bombshell"
GOAL:	Liberation from overpowering inner images and obsessions, breakthrough to freedom
RISK:	Failure, collapse
FEELING IN LIFE:	Phases of upheaval, insecurity and surprising changes, and liberation

THE STAR .

ur hero has finally reached the water of life. Its secret is not the quality of the water, but the difficulty of finding it. As in Fantasia, the underworld of the "Neverending Story," it is always located "on its borders." But since Fantasia, like the unconscious, is boundless, these must be inner boundaries that have previously confined us. Now, after the prison walls have been blown up, and the dust has settled, the liberated soul sighs in relief and gathers new hope. After having long been imprisoned in the tower of false consciousness, it joyfully feels a freedom it has never known. In the expansiveness of this freedom, a great future full of unsuspected perceptiveness can be seen. This happy feeling of boundless freedom can be heard in Dante's words as he leaves the Inferno: "Thence issuing we again beheld the stars."[1]

The Star
The Fountain of Youth

In the tale of Amor (Cupid) and Psyche, this mysterious water is also involved. It is the third task that the angry Aphrodite demands of Psyche, who desperately searches for her lover. She must fill a crystal container at an unreachable spring guarded by dangerous snakes, which is fed by the underworld rivers Styx and Cocythos. In Psyche's completely hopeless position, the eagle belonging to Zeus, the king of the gods, helps her. Zeus still owes Amor, her beloved, a favor. So this story also proves to have the connection with the animus as an essential key to the solution. "But the unique feature of Psyche's development is," according to Erich Neumann, "that she achieves her mission not directly, but indirectly, that she performs her labors with the help of the masculine, but not as a masculine being. For even though she is compelled to build up the masculine side of her nature, she remains true to her womanhood."[2]

The tarot card shows many oracle symbols which stand for a look at the future and therefore simultaneously for the wisdom of the cosmos. The stars naturally point to astrology. Their number and the eight rays call to mind the symbolism of the number eight, which is the mediator number between above and below, between Heaven and

[1] Dante, *The Divine Comedy*, Inferno (New York: Doubleday, 1947), Song 34, Verse 139.
[2] Erich Neumann, *Amor and Psyche* (New York: Bollingen Foundation and Pantheon Books, 1956), p. 110.

Virgil and Dante after leaving the underworld. "Thence issuing we again beheld the stars." (Woodcut by Gustave Doré).

Earth. The bird on the tree can be understood as an indication of the bird-flight oracle. Above all, in ancient times migratory birds were considered messengers of the heavens since they listened to the council of the gods in winter. The augurs could then read what the gods had decided for the coming year from their formation and behavior when flying back in spring. Birds also symbolize the visionary abilities of the deities to whom they belong. For example, the ibis is the bird of Thoth, the Egyptian God of Wisdom; the two ravens Hugin and Munin, accompany the Germanic god Odin (see page 83); and naturally the cranes are the birds of Apollo, the oracle god of Delphi.

The tree stands for developed wisdom, and was both the basis of the calendar as well as for prognoses of the future in Celtic tree astrology. All of these oracles pronounce the cosmic law and can open a view of the future. And this is precisely the main significance of the card. It is as if the hero's eyes have been opened, both the inner and the outer! A new future is revealed to him here. He can recognize the newly won possibilities, which he has opened up for himself through his heroic deed. As in a magnificent vision, he sees the path lying before him, leading him to the expansiveness of a horizon he had never imagined.

The naked figure on the card is the embodiment of Binah, the Cabalistic principle (sephiroth) of higher reason. Here she pours out the water of life, both into the water and onto the land. Water makes the earth fertile and is therefore an expression of a connection essential to life, whereby pouring the water into the water is an expression of abundance. As a result, this card opens our eyes to cosmic law and a joyful future in which the abundant water of life flows to us from the starry heights; considerably more than we need.

Moreover, this insight into the cosmic order, this premonition of eternity, can evoke the new consciousness of time that already dawned at the 14th card (see page 144). When the tower of false consciousness is smashed to pieces, all the upside-down concepts of a solely quantitative, linear form of time made of the past, present, and future collapse. Freed from the constriction of the old consciousness, we understand here how one-sided and false our understanding of time was, how hopelessly we have chased after pure illusions. "Unable to live in the timeless present and bathe in the delights of eternity, we seek as anemic substitutes the mere promises of time, hoping always that the future will bring what the slender present so piteously lacks."[3] This

---

[3] Ken Wilber, *No Boundary* (Boston: Shambhala, 1981), p. 64.

Figure 49. Dike watches over the laws of this world (Justice), while Themes personifies the laws of the cosmos (The Star).

leap of consciousness is like bathing in the fountain of youth. It saves us from being fixed on time and gives us the gift of boundless freedom from time. It is the deep understanding that Siddhartha found toward the end of his journey, when he learned from the river that there is no time at all; the river is everywhere at the same time, at the source and at the mouth, at the waterfall, at the ferry, at the current, in the ocean and in the mountains—everywhere at the same time. Only the present exists for it, not the shadow of the past, nor the shadow of the future.[4]

Through its cross sum, The Star (XVII) is connected with Justice (VIII), if we maintain the original numbering of this card. While the hero learned the laws of the world at the eighth stage, he or she now comprehends the laws of the cosmos and gains insight into much larger, more universal correlations. In the Greek world of the gods, these interconnected principles were embodied by the goddess Themis and her daughter Dike. Themis, the daughter of Uranus (Heaven) and Gaia (Earth) is a personification of eternal order and justice. She corresponds with the themes of The Star, especially since the oracle at Delphi belonged to her until Apollo took it over at a later time (figure 49). On the other hand, her daughter Dike, who is depicted on Justice, was considered to be the goddess who ensures there is justice on Earth with her sword, which has been sharpened by fate.

---

[4] Cf. Hermann Hesse, *Siddhartha* (New York: New Directions, 1951), p. 107.

Keywords for THE STAR

ARCHETYPE:	Wisdom
TASK:	Gaining hope, vision of a new future
GOAL:	Understanding the bigger picture, gaining insight into the wisdom of the cosmos
RISK:	Overlooking the present because of preoccupation with the future, being taken in by a will-'o-the-wisp
FEELING IN LIFE:	Trust in the future, feeling young and refreshed

he path led the hero through ten stages, which correspond to the astrological symbolism of the five planets—Mercury, Venus, Mars, Jupiter, and Saturn—in both of their aspects. These are the cards from Temperance (XIV) to The Moon (XVIII) and the cards related through the cross sum, The Hierophant (V) to The Hermit (IX), which embody the respective polarities of these planets in a vivid manner (see figure 50 on page 192).

Mercury (☿), the God of Roads, who was also known in Greek mythology as Hermes Psychopompos, which means he was known as the guide of souls, and is shown in the Hierophant (V) as the educator and guide in the outer world, and in Temperance (XIV) as the actual guide of souls through the night.

Venus (♀), the Goddess of Love, is reflected by The Lovers in her light aspect. Her dark pole is shown in the passionate entanglement of The Devil.

The Moon
The Dangerous Return

Mars (♂) demonstrates his springtime power in the departure of the hero on The Chariot (VII), whereby The Tower (XVI) reflects his overturning force, but primarily his warlike and destructive aspect, which can lead to either ruin or breakthrough.

In classical antiquity, Jupiter (♃) was considered to be the highest judge over gods and human beings, in Heaven and on Earth. This is expressed in Justice (VIII), which stands for the laws of the world, as well as The Star, the symbol of the laws and wisdom of the cosmos. Jupiter was the spouse of Themis, who corresponds with The Star as the Goddess of Heavenly Justice. Their mutual daughter Dike (Roman: Justitia), the Goddess of Earthly Justice, can be seen on Justice. Like her, Jupiter was also frequently depicted with a scale in his hand.

In its light aspect, Saturn (♄) shows himself as the wise old man in The Hermit (IX), whereby his difficult side that lets fear arise from constriction corresponds to The Moon (XVIII). And this card represents the last test on the path.

However, the work has still not been completed. Although the monster has been overcome, and the imprisoned soul freed, the hero still has the difficult return ahead. He or she must find the way out

Figure 50. The cards Temperance to The Moon and the cards that are related to these through their cross sum, The Hierophant to The Hermit, reflect the two aspects of the planets Mercury to Saturn respectively.

and should not lose the way in the labyrinth of the underworld. Insidious dangers lurk on this return route and become traps for great failed heroes. This is where Orpheus turned around and lost Eurydice forever.

This is also where Lot's wife turned around and was changed into a pillar of salt forever. Psyche had already obtained Persephone's beauty ointment, but could not resist the temptation of opening the jar despite all the warnings, and fell into a sleep of death. Gilgamesh had even found the herb of immortality—the new understanding of time, the consciousness of eternity from the previous card—on his journey to the other world. However, as he briefly let go of the plant on his return journey in order to drink water from a fountain, the snake came and ate it.

The laws of the underworld are strict: anyone who eats there, even if this is just one seed of a pomegranate, is not permitted to return to the upper world. This is what happened to the kidnapped Persephone. Whoever sits down in Hades one single time, even if this is just for a brief moment, will sit forever like Theseus and Peirithoos on the footstools of forgetting, from which they will never again rise. All of this makes it clear that the descent into the underworld is a task that wants to be performed and should not become an end in itself. This corresponds with the fairy-tale motif of the enchanted forest in which the hero gets lost. There the hero is courted and enchanted by bewitching beings who want to seduce the hero into giving up the journey, betraying the magic word, or forgetting his (or her) name; precisely all the things that have been learned from The Hermit, the card related to The Moon by way of its cross sum. Here, at this point, is the greatest danger of forever losing in one blow everything that has been achieved with difficulty. The ancient Persian writer Nizami tells of this in the story of unrequited love in a manner that is unsurpassed in beauty and tragedy, and is impressively told in his fairy-tale collection by the Indian Princess on a Saturday in the black Saturn dome.[1] It is too beautiful to tell it in words other than his own, and therefore too long to be repeated here.

This is also the tragedy of the Nibelungs, which can be described on the basis of the last tarot cards. Siegfried has mastered the previous stages with bravado. He courageously went into the cave where Fafnir watched over the treasure of the Rhine (The Devil), fought with this dragon and conquered it (The Tower). The bath in the dragon's blood

Orpheus grieves for his lost Eurydice (Alexandre Seon, Musee d'Orsay, Paris).

---

[1] Cf. Nizami, *The Story of the Seven Princesses* (London: Cassirer, 1976), p. 7ff.

Gilgamesh (?) with the immortality herb, which he lost to the snake on the return route (Relief from the palace of Ashur-nasier-apal II in Nimrud, Metropolitan Museum of Art, New York).

made Siegfried inviolable. When he ate from the dragon's heart, his eyes and ears opened up. He understood the language of the birds and saw Bruenhilde, his anima, in a vision. He promised to free her from the fortress of flames and marry her (The Star). But then he unsuspectingly partook of the drink of forgetfulness, which had been mixed for him at the court of King Gunter (The Moon). Because of it, he forgot the beautiful Valkyrie and married Kriemhild. With this betrayal of his anima, his demise was sealed.

Translated to everyday life, these images mean that the encounter with the powers of the unconscious can be dangerous, and only a strongly developed consciousness has enough strength to avoid being swallowed by the unconscious. The danger of the descent into the underworld leading to withdrawal from the world is great because the following can quickly occur: the actual, real world is neglected and forgotten since the flood of images from the unconscious is so intoxicating, so much more beautiful, and so dreamlike in the truest sense of the word. Even Homer warned of the danger of being led into insanity by the powers of the unconscious when he spoke of the two gates of the dreamland. One is made of horn, the other of ivory. The true dreams come from the first one, and the false dreams come from the other.

This ambivalence is also a reason why the ancient mystery schools were not available to just anyone, but placed high demands on the maturity of the aspirants. In contrast to this, esoteric knowledge is accessible to practically anyone today, even though some information is watered down and true esoteric knowledge is pushed to the edges by superficial hocus-pocus. There, in seclusion, it can best blossom. But those who feel attracted to the most simple and comfortable explanations possible and consider them to be the secret knowledge according to which they orient their lives should ask themselves whether they are joyfully engaging in a withdrawal from the world, which will sooner or later strand them in an enchanted forest, from which it will be hard to find a way out.

Similar experiences are also found in other areas. One example is self-improvement groups. As indisputably valuable as their services may be, it is also questionable when one finds a hard core of partici-pants in these groups who move continuously from one group to the next. These people no longer want to return to everyday life, which they often experience as being hostile. They have confused the worlds and no longer want to do without the feeling of "family" that their groups give them. They sit on the footstools of forgetting, have gotten lost in the labyrinth of the underworld, and no longer know their true names. They have forgotten what they actually wanted, why they orig-inally set out: namely, to have important experiences in the group in order to subsequently integrate these into the real world of everyday life. This is why Jung also warns: "If our psychology is forced . . . to stress the importance of the unconscious, that does not in any way diminish the importance of the conscious mind. It is merely the one-sided over-valuation of the latter that has to be checked by a certain relativization of values. But this relativization should not be carried so far that the ego is completely fascinated and overpowered by the archetypal truths. The ego lives in space and time and must adapt itself to their laws if it is to exist at all."[2]

The tarot card shows a crab emerging from the water. It can also be understood as an indication that the Tropic of Cancer has been reached, whereby The Hermit, with his Saturn/Capricorn correlation stands on the Tropic of Capricorn (see figure 51 on page 196). The sun, the heavenly role model of all heroes must reverse directions at these two points every year. The same applies to the heroes, who cross a threshold at both points. If the journey through the night started after The Hermit with the double-digit cards, The Moon means emerging from the watery depths and returning to the light. Since ancient times, Saturn, who astrologically corresponds with this card, has been seen as the guardian of this threshold.

The Moon card is frequently misunderstood today because we primarily connect the moon with romantic images. But here it means darkness, night, and the deep exploration of the inner spaces. The Moon has pushed itself in front of the sun and darkened the light (= eclipse of the sun), a natural phenomenon that was usually considered

---

[2] C. G. Jung, "Psychology of the Transference," in *The Practice of Psychotherapy*, CW, vol. 16, ¶ 502.

Figure 51. The Tropic of Cancer and Tropic of Capricorn. The sun (and hero) must turn around at these points.

to be a bringer of misfortune and has always been experienced with fear and unease.[3] The card shows a ford, the place of a possible crossing that is always dangerous, and a narrow path that leads to the gray towers, which were first seen on Death. They are the heralds of the heavenly Jerusalem, symbol of the highest good we can attain (see figure 52).

However, the path there is difficult and dangerous. It is guarded by a dog and a wolf. While the dog (as already seen on The Fool) represents the friendly and helpful forces of the instincts, the wolf embodies their dangerous and destructive aspects. It corresponds with Cerberus, the hell-hound of Greek mythology, whose task it is to make sure no soul escapes from the underworld. Although the goal, the place of redemption, the heavenly Jerusalem, is already within reach, an extremely difficult tightrope walk must be survived. "But the gate to life is narrow and the way that leads to it is hard, and there are few people who find it" says the Bible at the end of the Sermon on the Mount (Matthew 7:14). In medieval pictures, this stage is often depicted as a narrow bridge that the souls must cross in order to reach eternal life. At this point, fairy tales tell of the balancing act the hero must accomplish in order to overcome an abyss or a narrow pass, the last threshold on the edge of a sword.

---

3 Although this interpretation is unusual, it not only completely corresponds with the correlative meaning of this card, but is also suggested by its number. The number 18 represents eclipses in as far as all eclipses of the Sun and Moon repeat after a period of 18 years, the so-called Saros Cycle, in the same order.

DEATH.

THE MOON.

Figure 52. The two towers, behind which the rising sun can be seen, on the Death card are an indication that the journey through the underworld will lead to a new sunrise. The towers, as heralds of the heavenly Jerusalem, have almost been reached on The Moon card. But the light cannot be seen yet because the moon has pushed itself in front of the sun.

The corresponding danger on the path of the hero lies in becoming enslaved to the dark aspect of the anima, and therefore being led into lunacy by the inner female guide. Particularly as it is the actual nature of the unconscious to be bipolar and ambivalent, the guide of souls also behaves in quite a paradox manner. In the Parzival legend, the anima splits off into a light aspect and a dark aspect, for example, the red star woman and her dark counterpart, the bringer of bad fortune, "la pucelle de malaire." These two correspond to The Star and The Moon (see figure 53 on page 199). On the path to self-development, it is imperative to comprehend at this point that it is not the anima, herself, that is the goal, but that she wants to lead us to a wholeness beyond herself, just as Beatrice guided Dante over the Mount of Purgatory to the view of the Highest.

As long as the hero is fascinated by the light side of his anima, the star woman, he will also remain enslaved to her dark aspect. This dark aspect has pushed itself in front of the sun here as the moon. Only when the hero recognizes that the actual goal, the sun (as a symbols of the self), lies *behind* this darkness, can he escape from the labyrinth, or the enchanted woods. In her interpretation of the Parzival legend, Emma Jung describes this difficult passage as follows:

> In point of fact, the anima behaves very paradoxically, or else she splits into two opposing figures, between which consciousness is torn this way and that, until the ego begins to concern itself with

The narrow bridge that leads to eternal life (fresco by Loreto Aprutino, Santa Maria, Italy).

the task of individuation. It is only when a man begins to have an apprehension of the Self behind the anima [the sun as the symbol of the self behind the moon, the dark aspect of the anima] that he finds the foundation on which he can escape her pulling and tugging in contrary directions. On the other hand, as long as she is entangled with the image of the Self, he cannot escape from her trickery, for she wishes to enmesh him in life, and at the same time to pull him out of it, to enlighten and deceive him, until he has found both himself and an inner basis beyond the play of the paradoxes.[4]

Fear and constriction are two closely related words. Astrology connects these experiences with the planet Saturn, the guardian of the threshold. Saturn is considered to be the wise old man, as shown on The Hermit (XI). But the card associated with The Hermit by way of its cross sum, The Moon (XVIII), corresponds with the threshold that Saturn guards. It is the threshold of fear. It exists everywhere in the outside world where we must do something unfamiliar and enter into

---

[4] Emma Jung and Marie-Louise von Franz, *The Grail Legend* (New York: Putnam, 1970), p. 262. Brackets mine.

a new land. But we also experience it at least as intensely within as soon as we enter into the world of The Hermit. Many people become afraid when they are suddenly totally alone in the stillness of a secluded place. At night, without any recognizable external reason, this fear can even take on panic-like characteristics. Seen in psychological terms, this is the fear of the unconscious that forces its way through the threshold of consciousness, from which we run away to the extent that we flee from stillness and loneliness.

C. G. Jung once compared the modern person with a house owner who hears an inexplicable sound at night that is coming from the cellar. In order to calm himself, he goes up to the attic, turns on the light there, and discovers that it wasn't anything at all. Going to the attic, which means "into the head," and explaining away everything that could make us afraid is easy. On the other hand, going into the cellar, into the rooms that are dark, musty, and smell like mold, triggers an oppressive feeling, and is difficult for us because we encounter our dark side here. This is why we constantly divert ourselves in everyday life so that our vital energy flows into external objects. But when we are alone and in the stillness, it flows into the unconscious and activates all the contents that we had already suppressed so "beautifully."

In the myths of many peoples, including the Upanishads of India, the moon is considered the gateway to the heavenly world. To the same extent that the goal lies behind Saturn's threshold, the most enriching and delightful experiences that can be achieved lie behind

Figure 53. The star woman and the black moon as the light and dark polarity of the anima. Only the hero, who recognizes the sun (as symbol of the self) behind the moon, can attain the goal.

Top: Warned by Circe, Odysseus succeeds in resisting the temptations of the death-bringing sirens (vase, British Museum, London).

Bottom: Theseus conquers the Minotaur in the labyrinth of Crete. However, he only finds the way back because he was connected to Ariadne's thread (vase, British Museum, London).

the fear. This is why Saturnian rituals, such as fasting, silence, and aloneness, belong to all religions as the transitional rituals that help the human being cross this threshold. Even if it can mean darkness and fear, The Moon card should not be seen as a "bad" card, or as an indication that we should avoid something. The task here is to not lose heart, not to become discouraged by the darkness, but to follow the longing and sincerely take the path of fear with courage and trust in order to reach what is authentic behind it. In such frightening situations, psychology advises us to express the unconscious by letting it speak. This is perhaps one of the reasons that people who live in seclusion frequently talk to themselves.

As we know, Odysseus also had considerable problems with his return. He had almost reached his home island of Ithaca twice, but each time his companions (the nonintegrated aspects of his personality[5]) made a mistake, and the ship was immediately driven out to sea by the raging winds or tides for a new odyssey. On his journey, which brought him back to "The Hanged Man" on more than one occasion, and constantly let him begin a nighttime sea journey anew, he heroically mastered the previous stages. But without Athene, his anima who also constantly rushed to help him in the form of Circe, Calypso, Leucothea, or Nausicaa, and who gave him decisive advice time and time again, he would have been lost. Without Circe's advice he would have resisted neither the deadly enticements of the Sirens that awaken longings, nor

---

[5] See "autonomous complexes" on page 161.

could he have overcome and survived the highly dangerous narrows between the monsters Scylla and Charybdis. And he certainly would never have returned to his homeland without the help and intercession of his protecting goddess, Athene.

Theseus was also in constant contact with his soul guide, Ariadne, as he pressed forward into the inside of the labyrinth in order to overcome the Minotaur there. It was she who gave him the thread, the other end of which she held in her own hands. Without this common bond, the hero would have been lost in the labyrinth, a symbol of the underworld. Without this help, he would never have been able to find the way back. This myth can be read from the perspective of both sexes. Without the constant connection to Ariadne, his anima, Theseus would have been lost forever. As for Ariadne, it would never have been possible to rescue her had she not been connected with Theseus, her animus, through the thread.

Right at the entrance to Hell, underworld judge Minos let Dante learn that it is a crucial decision when we decide to trust someone, and that it is easier to get into the underworld than to get out of it. He warns: "Look how thou enter here; beware in whom thou place thy trust; let not the entrance broad deceive thee to thy harm!"[6]

Even the oldest tradition that has been passed down to us of a resurrection contains the same motif. It is the magnificent epic of the ancient Sumerians that sings of the descent of their Queen of Heaven, Inanna, into the underworld.[7] It tells how Inanna, the Goddess of the Great Above, leaves her heavenly throne to find her dark sister Ereschkigal, the Goddess of the Great Below. However, before she knocks on the doors of the underworld, she takes decisive precautions. With her wise vizier Ninshubur, she discusses and agrees on what should be done if she does not return after three days, as planned. And she actually would have disappeared forever in the "land of no return" had not Ninshubur faithfully done everything that they had discussed beforehand. As a result, the return succeeds in this oldest myth of resurrection only because the heroine has allied herself with her vizier, her animus.

The guide of souls can also be understood as the power to maintain the proper and necessary relationship of tension between the various counterpoles: masculine and feminine, action and inaction, courage and discouragement, euphoria and depression, but above all,

---

[6] Dante, *The Divine Comedy*, Inferno (New York: Doubleday, 1947), Song 5, Verse 19.
[7] Cf. Diane Wolkenstein and Samuel Noah Kramer, *Inanna, Queen of Heaven and Earth: Her Stories and Hymns from Sumer* (New York: HarperCollins, 1983).

between moderation and immoderation. The journey through the night, diving into the depths of the unconscious, has led the hero to an enormous expansion of consciousness. The danger of losing everything at the last moment through a greedy maneuver by the ego, through betrayal or megalomania, is great. This is told by fairy tales, such as the one about the fisherman and his wife when the fisherman sets free a fish that he has already caught. As thanks for the fisherman's act of kindness, the fish promises him that it will fulfill his wishes. Urged on by his wife, his wishes increase each time until they finally end in megalomania, with the desire to be like God. The fish refuses the fulfillment of this wish and disappears, taking all the previous gifts with it. The fish that fulfills the wishes is a symbol of the self. The fisherman embodies an ego that is too weak, that lets itself be seduced by a negative anima aspect, an unconscious greed, into fulfilling wishes that become increasingly extreme. And since every ego dreams of becoming like God and immortal, an ego that is too weak cannot resist this temptation, becomes immoderate, and fails.

There is a great danger that the ego will consider transpersonal experiences as personal achievements, or identify with an archetype in the encounter with the images of the depths. The ego is always overwhelmed by an encounter with the self—or, expressed in different terms: wherever the ego is truly overwhelmed, it has encountered an aspect of the self. But then the decisive question is: "What does the ego do with this?" Does it become humble and put itself in the service of the greater whole? Or does it inflate itself in narcissistic megalomania, take credit for this encounter, feel itself to be chosen, boast of its enlightenment, succumb to fantasies of omnipotence, and thereby "blindly" give in to the guru sickness?

Within this context, C. G. Jung spoke of a mana personality.[8] He said that these bewitching powers are so irresistible for the ego that such a phase of ego inflation on the path of individuation is almost unavoidable.[9] But once it has been overcome, this mana phase appears rather embarrassing in retrospect. This is why it is important to know this from the start, so that the phase can be kept as brief as possible.

Here, at the end of the journey through the underworld, it becomes apparent whether the ego has maintained the proper attitude in the encounter with the powers of the self. In the fairy tale, Mother Holle decides at the exit of "hell" whether the heroine returns to the

---

[8] Mana is a Polynesian term for soul power.
[9] C. G. Jung, "The Relation between the Ego and the Unconscious," in *Two Essays on Analytical Psychology*, CW, vol. 7, ¶ 374–406.

upper world as the golden girl or the dirty girl. While the golden girl humbly serves the power of the self and fulfills the Saturnian tasks, the dirty girl is only concerned with using the magical power of the self to let her ego-addicted wishes be fulfilled in the most comfortable manner. A modern correlation to this attitude can be found in unrestrained "positive thinking" with which, like a plunderer, the ego attempts to exploit the magical power of the unconscious for itself. The price of this avarice is high. The dirty girl is the result at the end of it.

For the Western individual, the danger of failing because of this hunger for power is particularly high because we have made little effort in our culture to explore our inner spaces. As inexperienced as we are in this manner, we are all the more endangered in succumbing to the temptations and enticements that emanate from these unknown worlds. We tend to consider the unconscious purely from the aspect of utility in order to use it for our machinations. But here precisely is the danger that Marie-Louise von Franz warns of when she says:

> Every utilitarian approach to the unconscious, or just wanting to make use of it, has destructive effects, just as, we are now beginning to realize, it has in outer nature. For if we only exploit our forests, animals, and the minerals in the earth, then we disturb the biological balance and either we or later generations have to pay a very big bill.[10]

Bastian Balthasar Bux, the hero of *The Neverending Story*, also almost failed and would have remained in Fantasia, since this other world was ultimately so enticing to him. His ego was so inundated with desires for power and improving the world that there were suddenly only good reasons for him to remain in Fantasia. Only at the very last moment, and only through the decisive action of his ally Atreju, did he manage to return to this world. Once here, he encounters the bookseller Koreander, who he first encountered at the beginning of *The Neverending Story*. The bookseller admits that he is also a traveler of Fantasia and greets Bastian with the memorable words: "There are people who can never come to Fantasia[11] and there are people who can come but they remain there forever.[12] And then there are still some who go to Fantasia and return again. Just like you. And they make both worlds healthy!"[13]

---

10 Marie-Louise von Franz, *Individuation in Fairy Tales* (Boston: Shambhala, 1990), p. 36.
11 They get stuck at The Hanged Man.
12 They fail at The Moon.
13 Michael Ende, *The Neverending Story* (New York: Puffin Books, 1993), p. 426.

Figure 54. The highest heights of becoming conscious (The Hermit) combines with the deepest exploration of the unconscious depths (The Moon).

This is precisely what is important. It is naturally not the goal of the journey to simply exchange one world for the other. When we have only looked through the right eye for the first half of life and finally discover the left one, it would be rather absurd to now tape the right eye shut in order to look only through the left eye from now on. Just as we have two eyes in order to see in perspective, two ears to hear stereophonically, we also have a conscious and an unconscious side, a masculine and a feminine nature; we are an inner and an outer human being, we stand between the light and the shadow. To be whole and live both sides is the goal of the journey. Reconciling both sides is consequently the theme of the next card.

Through its cross sum, The Moon (XVIII) is connected with The Hermit (IX). If The Hermit shows the highest heights of becoming conscious, The Moon stands for the deepest exploration of our inner nature, our unconscious depths (see figure 54). At no point of the hero's journey is the danger greater when it comes to losing, betraying, or forgetting The Hermit's gift—the knowledge about the true name and the magic formula—than here in the depths of The Moon. However, at no other point of the journey is there a greater chance of finding the way to oneself (The Hermit) through the path of fear (The Moon) than at this threshold.

Keywords for THE MOON

ARCHETYPE:	The night, daybreak
TASK:	The tightrope walk, cautiously overcoming the threshold of fear, not getting lost or losing oneself
GOAL:	Return to the light
RISK:	Getting lost in the enchanted woods, missing the goal, becoming enslaved by fear.
FEELING IN LIFE:	Irritations and insecurity, nightmares, fears, yearning

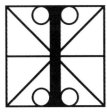

t is finished! The hero has won the victory. He has followed the path of the sun, crossed Heaven and Hell, passed all the tests, and truly returned again. This moment is like the rosy dawn. The darkness gives way and the soul emerges from the black spaces of the night to enter into the bright land of fearlessness.

This is the hour in which the monster must release the swallowed hero. Jonah is spit onto the land here, and the snake is forced to return the swallowed Argonaut, Jason, through the magic spell of Athene—Jason's anima.

The tarot card shows the hero visibly rejuvenated in childlike freshness, expressing a feeling of a new, sparkling morning after a long, dangerous, and dark night. Just as the Creation story in the Bible says "Evening passed and morning came—that was the first day"

The Sun
Return to the Light or Reconciliation

(Genesis 1:5), so the initiation, the true transformation of the hero, begins with the evening and now finishes with the morning.

When the hero appears to us as a child again at this point, it also becomes clear that the fruit of the journey is a refound simplicity. It lets a person who has fathomed and studied reality in its tremendous complexity come to a deep insight at the end of the path that all great truths are simple. However, immediately thinking that every shallow bit of nonsense is a deep truth would be just as foolish as the assumption that every simpleton is wise. "Human instinct knows that all great truth is simple. The man whose instincts are atrophied therefore supposes that it is found in cheap simplifications and platitudes; or, as a result of his disappointment, he falls into the opposite error of thinking that it must be as obscure and complicated as possible."[1]

We encounter The Fool from the beginning of the story in the child on The Sun card. He began his journey as a dumb fool, then soon became adult, very clear, and extremely competent. Here now, at the end of the path, he is once again humble, modest, and has become truly mature. Now he is the wise fool or the pure fool, as the Parzival

---

[1] C. G. Jung, "Richard Wilhelm: In Memoriam," in *The Spirit in Man, Art, and Literature*, CW, vol. 15, ¶ 91.

Jason is spit out by the snake and greeted by Athene, his anima (vase, Ruvo di Puglia, Jatta).

story calls him, who has returned to simplicity. So now he can find the Castle of the Holy Grail, which is only open to those with a pure heart. At the beginning of his journey, Parzival had completely fumbled his way into the castle unconsciously. But since he acted in a rather stupid manner, he was quickly thrown out again. Now, at the end of his journey, he can again find it as the pure fool and accomplish the work of redemption (see figure 55 on page 210).

A return to the original simplicity is also found at the end of Hermann Hesse's wonderfully told hero's journey of *Siddhartha*. At the beginning, he had also hoped to be able to avoid the abysses of life and find the path to enlightenment in a flight of fancy. However, he also had to learn that there are no shortcuts and we must deeply open up to life so that we can ultimately truly let go of it. Toward the end of his path, Siddhartha speaks as if he were describing the motif of this tarot card: "Now, he thought, that all these transitory things have slipped away from me again, I stand once more beneath the sun, as I once stood as a small child. Nothing is mine, I know nothing, I possess nothing, I have learned nothing." And a bit later, Hesse writes: "He was going backwards, and now he again stood empty and naked and ignorant in the world. But he did not grieve about it; no, he even felt a great desire to laugh, to laugh at himself, to laugh at this strange foolish world!"[2]

However, the rejuvenation of the hero also indicates a new consciousness of time that he has gained through his bath in the fountain of youth (The Star card). The insight into cosmic law has let him grow beyond the chronological experience of time, and has made him timeless in the best sense. Yet, in comparison to Gilgamesh, he has succeeded in bringing this consciousness of eternity over the threshold (The Moon). Here he now enjoys an inexhaustible wealth of time, similar to how he had experienced it as a child. If time had been a quantity for him of which he always had too little, he now experiences

---

2 Hermann Hesse, *Siddhartha* (New York: New Directions, 1951), p. 95.

its quality. Instead of running after it, in the hope of experiencing as *much* as possible, he now knows that the timeless feeling of a deeply experienced moment counts more than a thousand pursued pleasures; above all, we retain particularly rich memories of the phases of consciousness expansion.

The beginning and end of the path are similar to each other, but they are not the same. We have already seen this in the mandala, the inner and outer circles of which correspond to each other like Paradise Lost and Paradise Regained. Although they are similar, they are not identical (see page 62). Between them there is usually a long, difficult journey full of apparent detours that nothing can save us from. The great astrologer Oskar Adler found a beautiful allegory for this by comparing the life journey of a human being with the African Niger River, one of the longest in the world, even though it has its source just a few miles away from the ocean where it has its mouth. It must make a detour of many thousands of miles in order to reach its goal, which lies so near.[3]

However, our intellect, which wants to straighten out everything, finds such detours to be quite senseless. It would much rather take the direct route. As a result, people frequently come

The return to the light (Hieronymos Bosch, Doge Palace, Venice; photo: AKG, Berlin).

---

[3] Cf. Oskar Adler, *Das Testament der Astrologie*, vol. 3 (Munich: Hugendubel, 1991–1993), p. 350.

Figure 55. The naive fool at the beginning of the journey (The Fool); the pure fool at the end of the journey (The Sun); the white sun of The Fool has become "colorful" through the previous encounter with Death.

with huge expectations to a consultation in order to learn from the tarot cards, the I Ching, their horoscope, or a crystal ball what their next occupation should be, for example. In the process, they are not interested in recognizing the broad spectrum of possibilities with the help of this oracle, but seek a statement that is as narrow and fixed as possible, something like: "In two years you will be a blacksmith." The ego promises itself efficiency from such a prophecy. Instead of continuing to "incubate" the question, or sending off futile applications, the person could either take a trip around the world, or spend a little time studying various horseshoes and hoof sizes in order to prepare for the new occupation in this manner. This would be great, if there wasn't just one snag! A made-to-order occupation that just has to be picked up on Day One is as unlikely to exist as the perfect relationship that one day greets us completely readymade on our path. In order to reach these and other goals, we must grow to this point. The insecurities, doubts, and steps backward are just as much a part of this as all the difficult and apparently unnecessary detours.

> But the right way to wholeness is made up, unfortunately, of fateful detours and wrong turnings. It is a *longissima via*, not straight, but snakelike, a path that unites the opposites, reminding us of the guiding caduceus, a path whose labyrinthine twists and turns are not lacking in terrors.[4]

---

[4] C. G. Jung, "Introduction to Religious and Psychological Problems in Alchemy," in *Psychology and Alchemy*, CW, vol. 12, ¶ 6.

The same statement is made by Lady Aiuola in Michael Ende's *The Neverending Story,* when she says to Bastian:

> "You have taken the path of wishes and it is never straight. You have made a big detour, but it was *your* path. And do you know why? You belong to those who can only return when they have found the source from which the water of life comes. And this is the most secret place of Fantasia. There is no simple path there." And after a brief silence, she adds: "Every path that leads there was the right one in the end."[5]

?

In older tarot decks this card shows us a twin motif. It means the reconciliation of the two brothers who have been enemies, the reconciliation of light and shadow. Now that the hero has gone through both worlds to develop his light side and redeem his dark side, the reconciliation may take place.

This means that the decisive task on the feminine path through the double-digit cards has been fulfilled: the reconciliation of the civilized human being with his or her animalistic nature, the reconciliation between consciousness and its shadow aspects. This theme is shown right at the beginning in the card Strength, which opens this section of the path. But only after the overcoming (Death) and bursting of the boundaries (The Tower), which the ego had previously had to build for its development, can the reunification with the areas that have been split off and blocked out occur. The first step in this direction is symbolized by Temperance at the beginning of the nighttime sea journey with the mixing of the liquids that had previously been separated. Now that the night is over, the light of the new day shows that the unification has been successful and the human being has become whole. The sun at the end of the path has been reached (figure 56 on page 212).

In this reconciliation there also lies a decisive precondition for the "good" outcome of the story. Many traditions tell of this exciting

Hermes, the God of Roads, with the snake staff (caduceus) that binds the opposites, a symbol for the twists and turns of the path in life (Giovanni da Bologna, Florence).

---

5 Michael Ende, *The Neverending Story* (New York: Puffin Books, 1993), p. 446.

Figure 56. The unification with the neglected, dark, primitive, and scorned self as the task
(Strength); the mixture of the previously separated liquids as the beginning of the work
(Temperance); the successful reconciliation/unification (The Sun).

Figure 57. The Sun card in the Tarot of Marseilles.
The twin motif stands for the reconciliation of brothers who
have been enemies.

THE MAGICIAN.   WHEEL of FORTUNE.   THE SUN .

Figure 58. The mastery (The Magician); the task in life (Wheel of Fortune); the reconciliation of the opposites (The Sun).

encounter. A four-thousand-year-old ancient Babylonian epic tells us of Gilgamesh, the great powerful king of the city Uruk, who meets the wild Enkidu. The gods had created this giant solely for the purpose of restraining Gilgamesh's overbearingness. At their first encounter, the two immediately attack and fight each other: the civilizing power of the king against the animalistic wildness of the giant (equivalent to the two figures on Strength). At the end of their battle, Gilgamesh and Enkidu recognize that they are both equally strong, make friends with each other, and consider themselves brothers (see figure 57). Together they are unbeatable, so they set out and conquer the great enemy of the kingdom, the monster Chumbaba.

The same story is told about Parzival, who meets his half-brother Feirfeis at the end of his journey. The black Belakane, and their mutual father Gamuret, had conceived him in the Orient, which is why Feirfeis had a black-and-white checkered appearance. Parzival fought him, just as we are very quick to fight the foreign elements in our shadow. But there is also a reconciliation here of the embattled brothers as soon as they recognize that they are both equally strong. Because he no longer fights his shadow but recognizes his brother in it, with whom he reconciles himself, Parzival can now become the Grail King himself.

The duel between Parzival and Feirfeis,
which ends in the reconciliation between the embattled brothers
(Edmund von Wördle, Perceval Hall, Vinzentinum, Brixen).

Translated to the level of consciousness, this reconciliation also means overcoming the separation of the opposites with which the intellect splits reality. At this point, we comprehend why Jean Gebser says: "That which rationally appears to be an opposite is psychologically a polarity that, when we look at it, does not fall apart but which we are not permitted to destroy through rational dissection.[6]

The tarot connects these three cards (see figure 58 on page 213) with each other through the cross sum: The Sun (XIX), the Wheel of Fortune (X), and The Magician (I). This means that the task in life (Wheel of Fortune) that a person must master (The Magician) lies in the reconciliation (The Sun) of the opposites—the reconciliation of light and shadow, evening and morning, good and evil, civilization and wildness, man and woman, life and death. "Anyone who perceives his shadow and his light simultaneously sees himself from two sides and thus gets in the middle."[7]

Keywords for THE SUN

ARCHETYPE:	The day, the rosy dawn
TASK:	True reconciliation
GOAL:	Rebirth, wise insight, and mature modesty
RISK:	Being taken in by triteness
FEELING IN LIFE:	Carefree, sunny experiences, lightheartedness, joy in life

---

[6] Jean Gebser, *The Ever-Present Origin* (Athens, OH: Ohio University Press, 1985), p. 267.
[7] C. G. Jung, "Good and Evil in Analytical Psychology," in *Civilization in Transition*, CW, vol. 10, ₰ 872.

ow, after all the preconditions have been fulfilled, the wonder of transformation can occur. As the Parzival story reports, the place in which the work of redemption must be accomplished is only accessible to those who have a pure heart. It is the Castle of the Holy Grail, the heavenly Jerusalem, the Shambala, the city "Beautiful-to-See," the Buddhist's Pure Land of Amitabha, or whatever metaphor may be chosen in the various stories and cultures for the treasure that is so hard to find.

The treasure that the hero has fought for in the realm of the shadow, the elixir, the water of life, the blue flower, or whatever was so hard to find may be, can now bring healing. In most stories, this is quite a simple action, a kiss, a gesture, or just the right question that accomplishes the wonder of transformation. Whatever was unwhole or meant a calamity before is healed as a result. The shadow that lay over the kingdom disappears. The one who is bewitched turns into the enchanted prince or the freed princess. In the Parzival story, it is the incurably ill King Amfortas who becomes healthy at the moment that Parzival asks the right question. And this is quite simply: "Uncle, what is ailing you?" All these images show that the actual work is easy; however, this is true only when preconditions have been fulfilled. The actual work is always healing and becoming whole.

Judgement
The Healing

The Judgement card shows this wonder in the image of the resurrection. This is also a closer meaning of the card than its name implies. It has nothing to do with judgment in the sense of earthly jurisdiction. But it also does not depict Judgment Day, which is implied by the name of this card. However, the judgment over eternal life or eternal damnation is included in the themes of this card, since it is proved here whether the hero is a true hero or a swindler who has just cheated and possibly even robbed the hero of the treasure that is hard to find. "When the wrong person uses the right means," an ancient

Figure 59. In the Tarot of Marseilles, the meaning of Judgement becomes very clear: the divine trinity is freed from the dungeon of the earthly quaternity.

Parzival sees the Castle of the Holy Grail (Martin Wiegand, private collection, Munich. Photo: AKG, Berlin).

Chinese saying reminds us, "the right means then have the wrong effect." Every charlatan must fail at this point because only the true hero is successful at the work of redemption resulting from the motif of the ancient tarot cards. The resurrection flag on Archangel Gabriel's trumpet symbolizes overcoming the time of suffering and the victory over martyrdom. The three people who are being resurrected from the square grave embody the trinity, which is being freed from the quaternity (see figure 59 on page 217). Since the number three stands for the divine and the number four for the earthly, this picture says that what is authentic, essential, and divine is being liberated from the earthly dungeon.

This corresponds in fairy tales with the moment when the enchanted prince or the bewitched princess is freed from the false, ugly form and throws off the earthly armor, becoming visible as a radiant, divine nature. In the Waite Tarot, Waite has doubled the number of people and explained this with just a meager note: "It has been thought worth while to make this variation as illustrating the insufficiency of current explanations."[1] In any case, it is unfortunate that the symbolism, which had previously been so clear, is watered down as a result.

Through its cross sum, Judgement (XX) connects to The High Priestess (II), to which the cross sum of Strength (XI) also leads (figure 60). This link makes it clear that commitment and a will to life

---

[1] Arthur Edward Waite, *The Pictorial Key to the Tarot* (York Beach, ME: Samuel Weiser, 1973), p. 148.

Figure 60. Letting things happen and the knowledge of the right moment (The High Priestess); will to life and commitment (Strength); redemption, healing, and becoming whole (Judgement).

(Strength) are preconditions of redemption or healing (Judgement) that is, nevertheless, not the result of action, but rather of mercy that is dispensed when the preconditions are fulfilled and the right point in time has come (The High Priestess).

Keywords for JUDGEMENT

ARCHETYPE:	The wonder of transformation
TASK:	Redemption, liberation
GOAL:	Healing
RISK:	Failing as a cheat
FEELING IN LIFE:	Freeing oneself and feeling redeemed, finding peace of mind

W hoever completes the path has been completed. But this can, as Herbert Fritsche (a German occultist) said, "never be the person who has suppressed and inhibited his own nature but the one who has fulfilled it."[1] Our hero has reached the goal, found the lost paradise. The last card of the major arcana shows the "reversed Hanged Man" in the form of the dancing figure and thereby expresses that the standstill has turned into liveliness and that the person is now standing the right way (see figure 61 on page 222). The number four as the symbol of what is earthly is below in the form of the crossed legs, while the divine three is intimated by the open arm position. This is now above the four. As already seen on the 10th card, The Wheel of Fortune, in the four corners of the card are the four Cherubim as the four aspects of wholeness. They no longer

The World
The Paradise Regained

hold books in their hands, and therefore no longer dispense any lessons. All the lessons have been learned and the tests passed. The hero has become whole. He or she has found the path from the reversed world (The Hanged Man) into the right world (The World).

The same is expressed by the mandorla, which surrounds the dancing figure in the form of an ellipse.[2] While the circle with a middle point symbolizes the individual, the ellipse stands for a greater unity. According to the law of the circle, everything that emanates from its center point is reflected back to it by the border of the circle. This makes it a symbol of an ego that only relates the entire world to itself and experiences itself as the only middle point, around which everything else revolves. On the other hand, the ellipse is a "circle" that encloses two focal points. Its law says that every ray emanating from one of the focal points is reflected from the edge into the other focal points. This makes the ellipse the symbol of a greater unity, uniting the original pairs of opposites like masculine and feminine, light and shadow, conscious and unconscious within itself (see figure 62, page 222).

The Mythic Tarot shows the dancing figure to be androgynous, as an expression of the person who has accepted his or her inner oppo-

---

[1] Herbert Fritsche, *Der grosse Holunderbaum* (Goettingen: Burgdorf, 1982), p. 88.
[2] A mandorla is actually an almond-shaped halo of light, symbolic of the aura of the saint.

Figure 61. The return—the task—the goal.

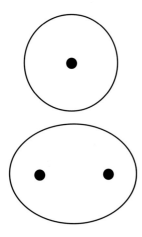

Figure 62. *Top:* The circle revolves around a middle point as the symbol of the ego. *Bottom:* The ellipse as a circle that encloses two focal points as the symbol of a unity that integrates the opposites.

site sexuality and, figuratively speaking, has become both sexes, and therefore whole (see figure 63).

In fairy tales, the image for becoming whole is found when the hero is crowned king at the end of the story. His soul guide has brought him to the crown that is concealed in the sun at the end of the path on the 14th card (figure 64).

In the *Divine Comedy,* it is Beatrice who guides Dante from the Mount of Purgatory to Paradise, up to the view of the Highest, the view of the eternal movement around a constant center.

This is not meant to give the impression that a point has been reached that is no longer of this world. "Wholeness is not so much *perfection* as *completeness*,"[3] emphasizes C. G. Jung and at the same time makes it clear that we have not separated ourselves from the earthly spheres at this point:

> [T]he united personality will never quite lose the painful sense of innate discord. Complete redemption from the sufferings of this world is and must

3 C. G. Jung, "Psychology of the Transference," in *The Practice of Psychotherapy*, CW, vol.16, ¶ 452. Italics mine.

Figure 63. The 21st card in the Mythic Tarot shows a dancing androgynous human being as the symbol of wholeness.

Figure 64. Temperance shows the guide of souls and a crown, concealed in the sun, at the end of the path.

Figure 65. Outer growth (The Empress) and inner growth (The Hanged Man) lead to wholeness (The World).

Dante is led by Beatrice, his anima, to the view of the Highest (Woodcut by Gustave Doré).

remain an illusion. The symbolical prototype of Christ's earthly life likewise ended, not in complacent bliss, but on the cross. . . . The goal is only important as an idea; the essential thing is the *opus* which leads us to the goal: *that* is the goal of a lifetime.[4]

---

[4] C. G. Jung, "Psychology of the Transference," CW, vol.15, ¶ 400.

Through its cross sum, The World (XXI) is connected with The Empress (III), to which the cross sum of The Hanged Man (XII) also leads (see figure 65 on page 223). This connection says that wholeness (The World) is only achieved where outer growth (The Empress) and inner growth (The Hanged Man) are in harmony.

If we look at the path of life as a spiral that gradually leads us to what is the Highest, then each turn on this spiral corresponds to one hero's journey. Seen in this manner, as long as we are traveling, we will return to all twenty-one stations over and over, yet—at least we hope—this will always be on a somewhat higher level. At the uppermost point of the path, but really only there, does this last card mean the unity of all things. However, this goal should be understood less as a final stage that must absolutely be reached, and more as an image that pushes us forward. As long as we reject or block out something within us or within Creation—whether this be Death and The Devil—or do not imperturbably consider it as something that is neither good nor bad, we are certain not to be at one with all things. And as long as this has not happened, the journey will start anew over and over again.

Bon voyage!

Keywords for THE WORLD

ARCHETYPE: Paradise regained

TASK: Arriving, taking one's place

GOAL: Standing properly, being at the right place, being whole

RISK: None

FEELING IN LIFE: Joy, deep satisfaction, having found one's home

Bibliography
and Recommended Literature

Astrology

Adler, Oskar. *Das Testament der Astrologie*, 4 vols. Munich: Hugendubel, 1991–1993.

Banzhaf, Hajo. *Der Mensch in seinen Elementen*. Munich: Goldmann, 1994.

Banzhaf, Hajo and Anna Haebler. *Key Words for Astrology*. York Beach, ME: Samuel Weiser, 1996.

Banzhaf, Hajo and Brigitte Theler. *Secrets of Love and Partnership*. York Beach, ME: Samuel Weiser, 1998.

Ethnology

Couliano, Ioan P. *Jenseits dieser Welt*. Munich: Diederichs, 1995.

Duerr, Hans Peter. *Sedna oder die Liebe zum Leben*. Frankfurt: Suhrkamp, 1984.

Literature and Poetry

Camus, Albert. *The Fall*. New York: Random House, 1991.

Dante, Alighieri. *The Divine Comedy*. New York: Doubleday, 1947.

Ende, Michael. *The Neverending Story*. New York: Puffin Books, 1993.

von Eschenbach, Wolfram. *Parzival*. Helen M. Mustard and Charles E. Passage, trans. New York: Vintage, 1961.

Hesse, Hermann. *Siddhartha*. New York: New Directions, 1951.

Religion, Mythology, and Fairy Tales

Bellinger, Gerhard J. *Knaur's grosser Religionsfuehrer*. Munich: Knaur, 1990.

———. *Knaur's Lexikon der Mythology*. Munich: Knaur, 1989.

The Holy Bible. London & New York: Oxford University Press, n.d.

Burkert, Walter. *Ancient Mystery Cults*. Cambridge: Harvard University Press, 1988.

Chuang Tsu. *Das wahre Buch vom südlichen Blutenland*. Munich: Diederichs, 1969.

Denzinger, Wolfgang J. *Die zwoelf Aufgaben der Herakles im Tierkreis*. Munich: Hugendubel, 1994.

Diederichs, Ulf (ed.) *Germanische Goetterlehre*. Munich: Diederichs, 1984.

Giani, Leo Maria. *Heilige Leidenschaften*. Munich: Koesel, 1994.

———. *Die Welt des Heiligen*. Munich: Koesel, 1997.

Godwin, Malcom. *Angels: An Endangered Species*. New York: Simon & Schuster 1990.

Grant, Michael and John Hazel. *Who's Who in Classical Mythology*. London: Oxford University Press, 1993.

Graves, Robert. *The Greek Myths*. London: Cassell, 1981; and New York: Doubleday, 1981.

———. *Hebrew Myths: The Book of Genesis*. New York: Doubleday, 1963.

———. *The White Goddess*. London: Faber, 1977; and New York: Farrar, Straus & Giroux, 1997.

Grimm's Tales for Young and Old. Ralph Manheim, trans. New York: Doubleday, 1977.

Holzapfel, Otto. *Lexikon abendlaendischer Mythologie*. Freiburg: Herder, 1993.

Kerényi, Karl. *Die Mythologie der Griechen*, 2 vols. Munich: DTV, 1966.

Koneckis, Ralf. *Mythen und Maerchen*. Stuttgart: Franckh-Kosmos, 1994.

Langyel, Lancelor. *Le Secret des Celtes*. Forcalquier, France: Robert Morel Editeur, 1969.

Lao Tzu. *Tao Te Ching*. Ch'u Ta-Kao, trans. London: Allen & Unwin, 1917.

Nizami. *The Story of the Seven Princesses*. London: Cassirer, 1976.

Pleister, Wolfgang and Wolfgang Schild. *Recht und Gerechtigkeit im Spiegel der europaeischen Kunst*. Cologne: DuMont, 1988.

Tetzner, Reiner. *Germanische Heldensagen*. Stuttgart: Reclam, 1996.

Weidelener, Herman. *Die Goetter in uns*. Munich: Goldmann, 1987.

Wolkstein, Diane and Samuel Noah Kramer. *Inanna, Queen of Heaven and Earth: Her Stories and Hymns from Sumer*. New York: HarperCollins, 1983.

Zimmer, Heinrich. *The King and the Corpse: Tales of the Soul's Conquest of Evil*. Joseph Campbell, ed. Bollingen Series XI. New York: Pantheon, 1948.

Psychology and Philosophy

Banzhaf, Hajo. *Der Mensch in seinen Elementen*. Munich: Goldmann, 1994.

Barz, Helmut. *Maennersache*. Zurich: Kreuz, 1984.

Campbell, Joseph. *The Hero with a Thousand Faces*. Bollingen Series XVII. New York: Pantheon, 1949.

Canetti, Elias. *Crowds and Power*. New York: Noonday Press, 1984.

Dürckheim, Karlfried Graf. *Meditieren—wozu und wie*, Freiburg: Herder, 1976.

von Franz, Marie-Louise. *Creation Myths*. Zurich: Spring, 1972.

———. *Individuation in Fairy Tales*. Boston: Shambhala, 1990.

———. *Shadow and Evil in Fairy Tales*. Zurich: Spring, 1974.

Fritsche, Herbert. *Der grosse Holunderbaum*. Goettingen: Burgdorf, 1982.

Gebser, Jean. *The Ever-Present Origin*. Athens, OH: Ohio University Press, 1985.

Gunturu, Vanamali. *The Play of God: Visions of the Life of Krishnamurti*. San Diego: Blue Dove, 1996.

Hornung, Erik. *Die Nachtfahrt der Sonne*. Munich: Artemis, 1991.

Hornung, Erik and Tilo Schabert. *Auferstehung und Unsterblichkeit*, Munich: Fink, 1993.

Jung, C. G. *Alchemical Studies*. Collected Works, vol. 13. R. F. C. Hull, trans. Bollingen Series XX. Princeton: Princeton University Press, 1967.

———. *Civilization in Transition*. Collected Works, vol. 10. R. F. C. Hull, trans. Bollingen Series XX. Princeton: Princeton University Press, 1964.

———. *Letters*, 2 vols. Bollingen Series LXXXXV. Princeton: Princeton University Press, 1974.

———. *The Practice of Psychotherapy*. Collected Works, vol. 16. R. F. C. Hull, trans. Bollingen Series XX. Princeton: Princeton University Press, 1954.

———. *Psychological Types*. Collected Works, vol. 6. Revision by R. F. C. Hull, H. G. Baynes, trans. Bollingen Series XX. Princeton: Princeton University Press, 1971.

———. *Psychology and Alchemy*. Collected Works, vol. 12. R. F. C. Hull, trans. Bollingen Series XX. Princeton: Princeton University Press, 1953.

———. *Psychology and Religion: West and East*. Collected Works, vol. 11. R. F. C. Hull, trans. Bollingen Series XX. Princeton: Princeton University Press, 1958.

———. *The Spirit in Man, Art, and Literature*. Collected Works. vol. 15. R. F. C. Hull, trans. Bollingen Series XX. Princeton: Princeton University Press, 1966.

———. *The Structure and Dynamics of the Psyche*. Collected Works, vol. 8. R. F. C. Hull, trans. Bollingen Series XX. Princeton: Princeton University Press, 1960.

———. *Two Essays on Analytical Psychology*. Collected Works, vol. 7. R. F. C. Hull, trans. Bollingen Series XX. Princeton: Princeton University Press, 1953, 1966.

Jung, C. G. and Richard Wilhelm, *The Secret of the Golden Flower*, Cary F. Baynes, trans. New York: Harcourt, Brace & Co., 1931.

Jung, Emma. *Anima and Animus*. New York: Spring, 1969.

Jung, Emma and Marie-Louise von Franz. *The Grail Legend*. New York: Putnam, 1970; published for the C. G. Jung Foundation for Analytical Psychology.

Mueller, Lutz. *Der Held*. Zurich: Kreuz, 1987.

———. *Magie: Tiefenpsychologischer Zugang zu den Geheimwissenschaften*. Stuttgart: Kreuz, 1989.

———. *Suche nach dem Zauberwort*. Stuttgart: Kreuz, 1986.

Neumann, Erich. *Amor and Psyche: The Psychogical Development of the Feminine*. Ralph Manheim, trans. Bollingen Series LIV. New York: Pantheon Books, 1956.

Orban, Peter. *Die Reise des Helden*. Munich: Koesel, 1983.

Remmler, Helmut. *Das Geheimnis der Sphinx*, Olten: Walter Verlag, 1988.

Watzlawick, Paul. *Vom Schlecten des Guten.* Munich: Piper, 1991.

Wehr, Gerhard. *Illustrated Biography of C. G. Jung.* Boston: Shambhala, 1990.

———. *Jung: A Biography*, D. M. Weeks, trans. Boston: Shambhala, 1988.

Wetering, Janwillem van de. *Zen Koan as a Means of Realizing Enlightenment.* Boston: Tuttle, 1994.

Wieland, Friedmann. *Die ungeladenen Goetter.* Munich: Koesel, 1986.

Wilber, Ken. *No Boundary.* Boston: Shambala, 1981.

———. *Up From Eden.* Wheaton, IL: Theosophical Publishing House, 1996.

Zaleski, Carol. *Otherworld Journeys.* New York and Oxford: Oxford University Press, 1988.

Symbolism

Becker, Udo. *Lexikon der Symbole.* Freiburg: Herder, 1992.

Biedermann, Hans. *Dictionary of Symbolism.* James Hulbert, trans. New York: Dutton, 1994.

Cooper, J. C. *An Illustrated Lexicon of Traditional Symbols.* London and New York: Thames & Hudson, 1987.

Miers, Horst E. *Lexikon des Geheimwissens.* Munich: Goldmann, 1987.

Tarot

Banzhaf, Hajo. *The Tarot Handbook.* Stamford, CT: U.S. Games Systems, 1993.

Banzhaf, Hajo. *Schluesselworte zum Tarot.* Munich: Goldmann, 1990.

Giles, Cynthia. *The Tarot.* New York: Paragon House, 1992.

Kopp, Sheldon B. *The Hanged Man.* Palo Alto, CA: Science and Behaviour Books, n.d.

Luginbuehl, Max. *Das Geheimnis des Dreikraeftespiels.* Pfullingen: Baum, 1961.

Nichols, Sallie. *Jung and Tarot.* York Beach, ME: Samuel Weiser, 1980.

Pollack, Rachel. *78 Degrees of Wisdom.* London: Aquarian, 1980.

Waite, Arthur Edward. *The Pictorial Key to the Tarot.* York Beach, ME: Samuel Weiser, 1973.

Index

HAJO BANZHAF teaches tarot and astrology, has published numerous articles in German magazines, and is the editor of the Kailash book series at Hugendubel Verlag, a well-known German publisher. Along with Brigitte Theler he has written *Secrets of Love and Partnership* (Weiser, 1998), and with Anna Haebler he wrote *Key Words for Astrology* (Weiser, 1996). He travels and teaches all over Europe and lives in Munich.

The Hero

THE FOOL.

The Path

DECISION

DEPARTURE

MATURATION

THE CHARIOT.

THE LOVERS.

THE

ONE'S
TRUE NAME

JUSTICE.

THE HERMIT.

THE CALLING

Daytime Arc of
Path of Consci

─ WEST ─

WHEEL of FORTUNE.

Maturation
Developing the Ego and
Overcoming the Ego

THE HELPFUL
ANIMAL

STRENGTH.

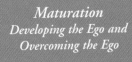

Nightly Arc of
Path through the

THE GREAT CRISIS

THE HANGED MAN.

DESCENT INTO THE UNDERWORLD

DEATH.

THE GUIDE OF SOULS

TEMPERANCE.

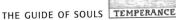

EDUCATION

THE HIEROPHANT

THE EARTHLY
FATHER

THE EMPEROR.

THE EARTHLY
MOTHER

THE EMPRESS.

the Sun
usness

THE HEAVENLY
MOTHER

THE HIGH PRIESTESS

Childhood
Gradual Development
of Consciousness

THE HEAVENLY
FATHER

EAST —

THE MAGICIAN.

Initiation
Experience of Self and
Self-Development

THE MOON.

THE DANGEROUS
RETURN

he Sun
Depths

THE STAR.

THE FOUNTAIN OF YOUTH

THE TOWER.

DRAMATIC LIBERATION

HE DEVIL . REALM OF THE SHADOW

The Return

THE SUN .

THE RECONCILIATION

JUDGEMENT.

THE HEALING

THE WORLD.

THE PARADISE REGAINED